FROM
SMOKE SIGNALS
TO
CELL PHONES

The Henry Laboucan Story

as told to

RITA MAKKANNAW

 FriesenPress

One Printers Way
Altona, MB R0G 0B0
Canada

www.friesenpress.com

Copyright © 2022 by Rita Makkannaw

Edited by Jan Simmonds
Reviewed by Erik Schou Hammerum

First Edition — 2022

All rights reserved.

No part of this publication may be reproduced in any form, or by any means, electronic or mechanical, including photocopying, recording, or any information browsing, storage, or retrieval system, without permission in writing from FriesenPress.

ISBN
978-1-03-913531-4 (Hardcover)
978-1-03-913530-7 (Paperback)
978-1-03-913532-1 (eBook)

1. BIOGRAPHY & AUTOBIOGRAPHY, NATIVE AMERICAN

Distributed to the trade by The Ingram Book Company

Dedicated to the wise ones and the coming faces

Table of Contents

Foreword ix

Part 1
Childhood 11

    Moss Bag Baby 13

    My first given name 15

    My second given name. 16

    Hudson Bay 18

    My Mother a Powerful Woman 20

    My Father 24

    My Grandmother 26

    My Grandfather Jean Marie Laboucan, Pepowakew 27

    Having a Child 31

    Raising a Child 33

    Burial Rites 35

    Governance 37

    Hunting 39

    Tea Dances and Ceremony 41

Part 2
Residential School 45

    Village suffering 47

    The kidnapping 50

    The Arrival to Torture 52

    Knocking Out the Priest 59

Part 3
The Raging Years 61

    Hatred 63

    Crazy Crees 65

    Bunky Willier 70

    Marriage 73

Part 4
Healing Journey 75

    Loon Lake Healing 77

    Peter O'Chiese 82

    Chief Smallboy 85

Elders 87

Basic Personality Types 94

The Eagle Teachings 97

Nature Teachings 100

Circle 102

Seven Power Centers 103

Indian Maiden's Legend 106

Part 5
Wanderings 109

Old Teepees 111

Symphony of nature 114

Turtle Teachings 117

Sundance 121

Willie Hamelin 130

Part 6
Professional Life 131

Affirmative Action Program 133

Universal Clock 140

Part 7
The Lubicon Struggle 147

    Newcomers 149

    Amnesty International Report 154

Part 8
Reflections 157

    True elder 158

    Popcorn elders 161

    Churchianity vs Christianity 164

    White Buffalo 169

    Prophesies 172

    Struggles 175

    Hear me See me Feel me 180

    Autumn years 190

Epilogue 193

Glossary of Aboriginal Traditional Terms and Protocols ... 195

Spiritual Objects 201

Glossary of political terms 203

Timeline 205

Foreword

Henry Laboucan was my buddy for over twenty years, and he is one of the most extraordinary people I have ever met. Residential school was a terrible nightmare and when he left his western education was very limited. After spending years in a rage, he realized that he had to make major changes. He set out on a mission to educate himself further in both the western and traditional way of his people. He became very well spoken and well read. He often spoke of his wish to share his teachings, but for many reasons he was somewhat reluctant. His reluctance to share stemmed from the fact that the Cree people are humble, and he did not want to appear to know more than anyone else. Partly because of the oppression they faced from the newcomers to their land. Partly because much of their old knowledge must be learned experientially by sitting with the elders over a long period of time.

In the end he felt it was important to share the history from a bush Cree person's perspective. Every family, every community differs a little in their teachings, but the foundations are all the same. (Connectedness, respect, humbleness, kindness and caring.) Constantly throughout the interviews Henry would say "That is the way I was taught." He would be very cautious to emphasize that these teachings were only his and he was not speaking for anyone else. He shared a history that everyone in this country we call Canada has a right and obligation to know. It is a very colourful history with many stories. Some will bring heartache, some joy and yet others will bring enlightenment for a way of life from which we can all learn.

Much of the old knowledge is being lost and he was one of the few people left here who was a 'moss bag baby.' He was born into the old traditions of communal teachings which began even before birth. Of that he was extremely proud. He saw the importance of sharing with his people who had lost their way and for the 'coming faces' the next generations. His life spans from traditional, before contact life, to the modern world of western education. It spans an age from horse and buggy to trucks and airplanes, from smoke signals to cell phones.

Part 1
Childhood

I was born in the bush, by Lubicon Lake in 1940, on tribal land which had belonged to my Cree ancestors since time immemorial. Lubicon Lake is situated very far North within the province of Alberta in western Canada. I was born free just like my people had been for thousands of years.

Later on, I came to see that this freedom was not to be taken for granted, and when they found oil reserves on my birth land, which in regards of amount and potential compares to those of Saudi Arabia, the land itself also noticed.

My story will not be about the oil industry, poisoned water, fleeing wildlife, or forest literally turned upside down, but about losing honor, beliefs, and pride. This is about my own healing journey, in my own life on this earth, from smoke signals to cellphones.

Moss Bag Baby

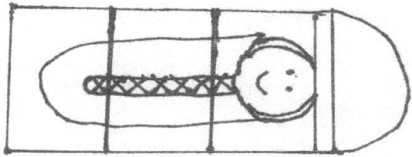

Waspison (Moss bag) with a cradle board

I was my mother's third and youngest son.

My first months in this life I lived in a moss bag that she made for me. I do not know how my moss bag was decorated. When she made it, she would have had a vision about my future and the type of person I would become, or she may have gone to an elder and brought tobacco and gifts to ask him or her what vision he or she saw for the future of the little guy. When finished, she would then wrap me tightly in my own wâspison (moss bag.)

Soon after my birth my mother would have returned to the trap line to snare rabbits and prepare the fur to wrap around the top part of my body. She would gather moss from the muskegs, as that was the softest and most absorbent and she would cover my little brown bottom with it, knowing moss also works against bacteria. It would have had a backboard and a willow was bent into an arc and attached to the backboard creating protection for my head. Sometimes the moss bags boards were made with willows around the chest area and the knees for more protection. I do not know whether mine was like that. I do not remember ever seeing it.

There I was, snug as a bug in a rug as she carried me on her back. I had the opportunity to see, smell and listen from my moss bag, and to learn with confidence.

When my mother was very busy on the trapline she would hang me in a tree while she was working, and she would always sing to me. Songs about life, the forest, the animals and how they helped us. When I became too heavy to be carried on her back, I would travel in the moss bag on her horse.

It was well understood that babies were very sensitive, and everybody would be very mindful about what was happening in baby's presence. No one would bring anguish or anger into a baby's life. If an adult was distraught, they would stay far away from a little one. Also, there was much respect for the information received from the little ones. If baby was fearful, the adults would get busy to find out immediately what made the little one afraid. Babies' reactions would never be ignored.

When I got older, my mothers, that is my birth mother and her sisters, would tell me the stories about my life before I could remember them. They would tell me all about how I would try to sing along with my mother, how inquisitive I was as I watched everyone at work. How I loved watching the leaves as they blew in the wind until I fell asleep. The moss bag brought the safety of the physical and the spiritual together, so I was not scattered. My well-developed instincts have their roots in the moss bag. That is how I knew very early who was kind, and who was not, when I first entered residential school at age seven.

Some native women still use the moss bag today. They do use diapers and wrap the babies tightly in a receiving blanket. When baby fusses for no apparent reason, moms will wrap the little one tight in their moss bag. Most homes with a baby will make a swing by putting two hooks in the ceiling and hang a looped rope from one to the other. A blanket would be folded around the rope creating a cradle, so baby in the moss bag can be placed in the blanket and rocked gently until they are sound asleep. Baby feels safe and cozy and will go to sleep within minutes. What's a few holes in the ceiling in comparison to a baby's well-being?

My first given name

In my culture we are all born into a certain clan or lodge. My lodge was the Thunder Lodge. My mother used to tell me stories about that.

Oonta Wahtaw was my first given name. It means wolf helper. Wolf teaches us family loyalty. All my life I was looking after my mother and my siblings the best I could. When it became too hard, I had to learn to let go. I guess my name was meant for me. I see that now.

We also had totems, but not the same as the west-coast people. They were smaller. When I was a child, some people showed them to me. I was told that my very gifted grandfather was at the top of the pole in the form of a thunderbird. I've never forgotten that. I can't remember who showed me that though. I was just a little guy. I rarely speak about my early name. I say it is too sacred to talk too much about.

My second given name.

One day the newcomers came up to our bush area. The RCMP moved in and became our local police. We called them 'yellow stripes' because they had yellow stripes on their pants. The priests also came in their long black robes. For me the 'yellow stripes' and the 'black robes' were so frightening. One day they came to our door, and I saw those colors, black and yellow. I think I was four years old. They came with orders from the Dominion of Canada and their God. They came to baptize the children and I was one of them.

When they came to the door, they barged right in. No consideration for our home. They kept saying the word "sauvage" Later I learned it meant savage in French and I would hear that word too much in the future.

Many children were baptized that day. At the time we didn't understand what the black robes were doing, but it was rough, and we were all crying. My mother tried to interfere but the yellow stripes held her down so she couldn't. Some of the adults in our village must have thought it was ok because they held us down. It was all so confusing for a little guy like me. I remember my mother screaming when the black robes came to take me away. She did not know what they were going to do to her son, and she was a mother bear trying to protect us all. The RCMP just held her down and they would not allow her to move. It took four women to hold me down. I would squirm and try to run away, but there were too many of them. You were supposed to bow over this big bowl. I didn't want to bow, and I didn't want those black robes to pour water over my head, but they made me bow and they poured water over my head anyway. I hated that and fought as much as my little brown body could, but those women were too strong for me. My mother tried everything to get to me. I just wanted my mom and both of us fought as hard as we could to get to each other.

After that we had friction in our community that had never existed before. Families of the baptized children were very upset with those four women who helped the aggressive newcomers do what they did. No one could understand why anyone would do that. I remember that so well even if I was just a little guy because I had never seen anything like that before.

In my culture we never used force. Before that day we had our ways of solving conflict. Never before do I remember the adults shouting and no one was manhandled. I guess that's why I still remember every detail.

When I went to residential school, the nuns and priests called me Henry and from that day forward that would be my name. I am now an old man and one day at pilgrimage suddenly this old fella called out my first-born name. Oonta Wahtaw was shocked that someone would remember.

Hudson Bay

The Hudson Bay established trading posts throughout the fur trading regions of Canada wherever the people gathered. I could not tell you my life's story without including The Bay, as we called it. Such is the impact it had on our lives and our culture for many years.

We lived just across from Cadotte Lake which is 84 kilometers northeast of Peace River. Cadotte Lake was a bit larger community than our village. There were approximately 40 people living there and Joe L'Hirondelle opened a store there. When we needed to go there, we travelled on a carved-out wagon trail.

Both our communities came from the Thunder Lodge, and I think we were the first to ever live on this land. No one knows for sure. We lived in a few cabins nuzzled together, surrounded by boreal forest with poplars, birch, and willows.

In 1670 King Charles II of England gave the Hudson Bay Company the right to trade wherever they wanted in most of Canada. The King didn't own the land. We did, but that was obviously not an issue to him at the time.

When the Bay moved into our little community, we were hunters and gatherers. Currency was non-existing therefore, when the Bay set up their post, trading furs for goods was most natural for us. I remember my grandfather being very proud of his felt hat, which would have come from this trading post.

England was hungry for furs and the Bay provided useful goods for us, such as pots, guns, axes, saws and machetes, beads and clothing, flour, and salt. They also brought in rakes to be pulled by horses and tools to cut the hay fields along the lake, which provided us with winter feed for our horses and more crops to trade. The Bay traders did not care about the pipe, our ceremonies, or our spirituality. We could not talk about those things, because they just didn't get it and some even thought we were crazy.

I heard the old people talk about life before the Bay and after the Bay. That was how we measured time. We would relate to major events. One unscrupulous Bay agent was not trading fairly for our furs, so one day he was summoned to come to our tribal meeting. When he showed up, we confronted him with his unfair practices in front of everyone. Public shaming was a big deterrent to bad behavior, and was he shamed! After that we demanded that the Bay send another agent, and they did.

My Mother a Powerful Woman

Julienne was my mother's baptismal name. Her Cree name was Kawenocht, or something like that. The old people always used that name. No one knows how she got that name for sure. The people who gave her that name would have finished their earth journey long ago.

My mother was born in 1903 into the Thunder Lodge. She was a powerful woman and a smart one. Although she was not very tall, she was big boned, and she looked powerful. She carried a sack of potatoes they called gunnysacks, 100 yards between the Bay and our vegetable shed, and it was not until I was 19 that I could do the same! Our little cabin was situated close to the Bay store. One corner was my mother's own place where she could cook. The other corner had an air-tight heater. We got those from the Bay. These heaters were so lightweight that we could easily take them to the traplines where we would live parts of the year. Our beds were willows or straw spread on the floor with a tarp or animal hides on top. They smelled so good. It was the outside brought into our house. Every time you moved you could hear the crunching of the straw. In the evenings my mother would tell us stories or sing us songs to the light of a bitch, which is a cloth soaked in fat. When lit, it would give us light and also a little heat.

I remember my mother's songs about her dreams for me. "Don't let my son grow up to be useless" she would sing, "He has a good mind and heart. Please guide him on his way." I know her words were made up as she went, but I have never forgotten. She taught us all the time about the animals and how they know what is good for them. It was from the animals we learned about medicines and what was good for us. She knew all about the different kinds of grasses and which ones were best for what. When there is no water around you use this special grass to clean your hands. Not all grass works for that. Some are too sharp and will cut your hands. Some grasses are good disinfectants some are great for stopping bleeding on a fresh wound. Some grass makes excellent pillows because it is soft. We just loved to romp around in the grass when we changed it for fresh now and again.

We also had another small shed which was filled with tools. When visitors came, we moved all the tools out and it served as a guest house. In those days we would always take real good care of all our visitors. We still do that today. They get the best food, and we look after them in every way. I loved it when people came because there was so much laughter in our house. Everyone always had a good time. People came from far and wide because they knew my grandfather had many good medicines and they knew he passed this knowledge on to his family.

We had another small cabin which was well insulated and served as a pantry. We stored all our food there. Our clothes were ragged but no one cared about that. Especially us kids because we were all the same.

I remember we had many horses. There were also wild horses grazing free. Somehow even if they all grazed together everyone knew which horses belonged to whom and everyone respected that.

We had a sleigh with a caboose to which my mother would hook up a horse and go and visit neighbors. We used to visit a lot in those days. Life was never boring. Then she would make a bed with grass and a bear rug on top. Us kids would go to sleep when we travelled a long way. Sometimes we would stay overnight with our friends and family. It was such fun to play with other kids.

My mother often used stories to teach us how to behave. She would tell stories about misbehavior of other children without naming anyone. That was her subtle way of teaching us about proper behavior and protocol. If we misbehaved, she would simply give us 'the look'. Somehow, we would always know what it meant. The elders of our community were the teachers of all us kids. My mother would bring gifts to them, and these wisdom keepers would teach about how to create harmony in our lives. My mother made sure I was taught properly and learned all I needed to carry on as a good man.

She would often talk about the guidance from the star people who live in the spirit world, our ancestors and our spirit guides. Star people send gifts like protection and wisdom, and they help us ease our suffering and guide us through challenges. She told me that no matter what I would face, the star people would be there for me if I asked for their guidance. I know I got protection from the star people. Many times, when I have faced challenges in my life, I would remember her words and ask for the help I needed. This is deep shshtuff.

We had very strict rules of behavior. The message was that the Creator created everything, so we must have reverence for all life, so to break a branch without using it was not allowed. If you do kill something and you are going to use it, fine. You say a prayer and follow protocol, but if you are not using it, you cannot break it, you cannot kill it. I heard that if a boy breaks a branch and does not use it, he may get beaten with it! I objected to this as a little guy, which meant I wanted to slap some guys and wanted to drop those principles, but the teachings would always come back and remind me.

Our family went everywhere together, to ceremonies, hunting, fishing, and visiting relatives. In summer, we used wagons to carry the children and goods needed for travel. We would put up our tent where we could all sleep.

We learned at an early age about the plants and herbs we needed as we helped mom pick them. My mother taught us to always pick enough berries and wild vegetables to share with the elders and those who could not get to the bush. She also picked medicine, which she used or traded with other medicine people. Hides would always be saved to make into rawhide. They would be stretched on wooden racks, dried, and softened and the hair removed with a scraper made of bone. Whenever the racks that she stretched the hides on had to be turned she would have to get help as they were very heavy. I remember helping her the best I could when I was little. Everyone would laugh because I was so small, but I tried. When I got bigger, I used to go hunting and would bring her hides. She tanned those hides until she was 88 years old.

My mother did arts and crafts from hides to make a living: moose hide gloves, moose hide jackets, sometimes decorated with shells or beads. She made head bands with our family emblem. She beaded moccasins and made beautiful traditional shirts. She did all that.

She would make crushed chokecherries which is very hard work as they are pounded and crushed, pit and all. She would set up a block of wood and cover it with a piece of hide and crush the berries with a rock. I am sure it was good for her soul as well as our stomachs. It has a nutty, fruity taste like nothing else I have ever tasted. We just had to be careful of the 'gravel' so we didn't break a tooth. It was delicious. Sometimes she would also make pemmican. That was made out of moose fat, crushed dried moose meat and blueberries or saskatoons.

When my mother was baking bannock she would sing a song about this young man who would turn into that big man who was a protector and a provider and would do good things. I was only a little fella and I wanted to be that man. No matter how busy she was, she would stop all her work and take time to talk to me. Now I am 76 and I have done everything that was included in that song.

It was my mom who taught me all about responsibility to all the people who came into my life. She told me to be a true man, a warrior, a defender, a protector of the old ones, the little ones and also the tribe. That is the code of life and that is a big one. That's a life commitment, to set moral and ethical principles, to be gentle and kind to all things and you have to behave like that always.

She taught me the female ways but not the female body. Everyone knew that women held the beauty ways. It was the men's responsibility to defend and protect them.

My mother always encouraged me never to forget who I was as a Nayhiyaw, (a Bush Cree person) and the blood line from which I came. I have done my best to live by her teachings. I'm not perfect, but I have tried.

My Father

My father did not have that sensitivity that my mother had, to touch your heart in a good way. He was a trapper, and he was always gone. When he did come home, he was in his own little world. He was kind of low until he was drinking. The Bay and others were selling liquor to him. He used to call me little bastard, because I was quick to pick things up and I learned things really fast, and that was a white man quality in his mind, so he called me little bastard. He had a horrible accent. A stupid accent when he spoke English. His voice was definitely created for Cree, and not English.

One time in our house, I do not know what happened, or why, but maybe jealousy came in my father's mind, and he took his rifle, a 3030, a pretty large rifle, and was going to do away with this little bastard once and for all. So, he aimed right at me, right at my heart, but he wobbled around so I knew his spirit was not with him. I don't recall fear at that moment, but disappointment for sure, and I was thinking, "If he kills me, I don't have to hear that word bastard anymore." When he pulled the trigger and shot, it felt like a sharp pressure on my head. When I looked in the mirror, I had gun powder all over my hair. He parted my hair with that bullet! Can you imagine the sight?

He dropped the rifle close to a bed. My mother came and she took away all the sharp objects in that house, knives, axes, guns, she hid everything. She forbade him to talk to us and she forbade him to ever again enter our house. "It is one thing to drink up our horses, our saddles, our wagons, but when you shoot at my son you are out!" My mother told him to take four horses and stay away from the family forever. He took six instead. When she noticed he had left with too many horses, she jumped on her horse and rode off at a gallop. In what seemed like a long time she returned, riding her horse, and held in her hand the other two horses that she considered ours.

My mother was very powerful, and if he would have touched her, she would have taken him down. Everybody in the community knew he shot me, and he became like an outcast after that. I did not see my father again for many years. I did hear he moved to Moccasin Flats in Peace River. Many of the people who took to the bottle moved there. It was a sick community because all the sick people who turned to alcohol gathered there.

I can honestly say that I did not miss my father much. We lived very well without him. I never called him my father since that day. I always called him Albut when I saw him later. I couldn't say Albert properly when I was a child, so it became Albut.

My Grandmother

All we ever called my grandmother was Kookum – her real name was never brought up in my presence. We never really go by names, but I know my grandfather's name was Jean Marie, and that's my middle name too.

From what I recall, Kookum was a very wise person. She knew all kinds of medicines, and she used to be a hunter. I lived with her in her tipi close to our cabin all summer. We had a little fire in the middle. We stayed until none of us could handle the cold and then we moved inside the cabin.

I was known to argue with her a lot! I had picked up certain words from the drunks. I guess I heard those words in the evening from another tipi. My grandmother wouldn't let me use certain words.

She would try to teach me, but I was too young to understand that deep truth. The community all said, "Henry is arguing with his grandmother again!"

Later on, she told me that she was training me to argue. As a little guy I wanted to be right, and she allowed it. She wanted me to be truthful, to not add things, and to stay by the truth.

Later on, I took care of her. She was too old to go hunting then. I was only eleven years old, and I had a gun, and I shot chickens, ducks, rabbits, and I took them home to her because after chewing moose hides for so many years her teeth were worn out and she could not chew dry moose meat anymore. That is why I got her chicken, rabbits and the ducks and she boiled the hell out of them.

My Grandfather Jean Marie Laboucan, Pepowakew

People still tell stories of my grandfather Jean Marie today.

My grandfather had two names, just like my mother, and the other name was Pepowakew. That is the way the old people pronounced. I was told that it means a special bird, not very big.

When the sky is high and blue, it flies high up. When it's going to rain it flies down really fast.

My grandfather was not very tall. People even used to call him Bug because he was just a little man.

People say he would be walking with some kids, making jokes, and playing around, and then suddenly he made a quick stop like he focused somewhere else. He instantly knew what was going on in Peerless Lake, 140 miles away. To drive there it would take about six hours, but he knew somebody was dying just then and that spirit came to say goodbye, and he knew that.

He was a man with total balance of body, mind, heart, and soul. People say he was the most balanced man, and he was said to be so clean inside so that you could not anger him, you could not hurt his feelings. His pure mind made him sensitive to the spirit world.

People came to him if they were sick or wanted information on what was to come. My grandfather did not need a shaking lodge to ask the spirits. (a shaking lodge is a ceremony where the spirits are called in for help.) He knew anyway, and he talked about the 'black robes' long before they arrived.

There was a story we heard many times about my grandfather. Once he was out looking for moose when he came across some blood on the ground, and he knew it was not from a moose. It was from a bear. Somebody had shot a mother bear and he followed the tracks. Suddenly he heard the sounds of three cubs, so say the people who remember those bears, and he took them home with him and raised them for three years and he learned from these bears.

I don't know how old he was when he found those cubs, but I heard he already had a son and by that I know he must have been older than 27 because we were never allowed to have children before we were 27 years old.

Spanish flu came with the black robes into our area in 1918, and what these bears told him was to get us a skunk. This little guy that sprays that smelly stuff on you. Yes, the bears told him, get us a skunk. Right under their tail is the stink bag, and he was told again by the bears to boil some water and mix four drops of that skunk stuff with some sweet and take it. Jean Marie did what the bears told him, and others did too. All who took that drink did not die from the Spanish flu, they were all okay. The people who said, I don't take that stuff, they died. The bears also told my grandfather to take a little of that skunk oil in a bag and hang it up by the door to save the house from the Spanish flu. There are still people in that area, who do that today, and they even drink it. Apparently, that flu bug could not handle that skunk oil! It saved me. If my mother would not have taken it, I would not have been here.

Eventually those bear cubs got so big that the people became afraid to come to his place. One day he decided to put the cubs in his boat and take them across the river. By this time, they had grown so big that he had to make two trips, so he loaded the two females up and made one trip and then came back for the male.

As long as he lived, the 'black robes' and the 'yellow stripes' never bothered us much and we could have our ceremonies and tea dances. He was so powerful, and they stayed away. After he passed, they slowly moved in on us and one day we too could go to jail for dancing, singing, drumming, and smoking our pipes.

Not only was he a healer but he was also what we call a 'dreamer,' who could foresee the future. Somehow, he saw what would happen when the Europeans would come, and he did his best to save land for his family. My mother told me that his dream was that his offspring and those of his brothers and sisters would live healthy and happy lives on our ancestral land.

Surveyors had begun to survey the land around Lubicon Lake. When he saw how the land was marked, he carved four totems, each depicting an animal. They were about 16 feet tall, and he erected them at the surveyors' stakes. He placed four smaller stakes in each direction around the totems. "This is our land," he told the Indian agents, LaRue and Liard. "My extended family members should also have land. This land is for my people," he said. "This is our traditional land." After all, generations of the Laboucan family had lived throughout the Buffalo Head Hills area.

He was the keeper of the family bundle holding sacred items used in ceremonies. This bundle dated back 16 generations which would put it back to the later 1400s. The bundle represented our family's past, and it was used in sacred ceremonies, where our ancestors were acknowledged.

I have been told that my grandfather was so powerful that he could levitate and that he could disappear, and then appear somewhere else. One must be very pure in thought and mind in order to do these things. I do not know of anyone today who is pure enough to do that.

When my grandfather Jean Marie had passed, people still came to give gifts for his memory. I remember people talking about how he did this, and he did that, he healed me, and so they came.

When we talk about my grandfather today, we often mention what we call a miracle happening long after his passing. One spring day when I was about fifteen years old, I came home to my mother to give her some money. That night our little cabin caught fire. We all escaped but tragically my mother's home burned to the ground. I remember my mother crying over the loss of the few belongings she had.

The next day when we returned to the site of the fire my mother began kicking at the remaining debris. Suddenly this picture was exposed among the ruins. Although scorched by the fire and the horse whose reins he was holding was burned, his image with the felt hat, his shirt and jacket, was unharmed.

I remember my mother preserved the picture in a small chest. Now the picture was the only tangible evidence remaining from her safe and peaceful childhood. The family believes there must have been a reason his image survived. Could it be it was a reminder for us that Jean Marie's vision was yet not fulfilled?

My Grandfather, Jean Marie, Pepowakew

My relations, Melvin Laboucan, Billy Thomas and Musqua recently ventured back to Lubican Lake, and they told me they not only found the old stakes their grandfather carved to save the land for his family, but they also found the old gravesites with the little, tiny cabins covering them. Long ago when we did farewell ceremonies, we covered the graves with a tiny dwelling. It was a reminder of the deceased person's life here on earth. That is the physical meaning. The cabins were small because they did not need them in the afterlife, where they were now home.

When I go up north today, people still talk to me about him, and they still think my grandfather is around. He knew things that nobody else knew. That is what the people say. But it puts me on the spot because I am nowhere near what he was!

I instinctively know some of what he knew – I never met him in life, but I met him in spirit. That is why I have blood memory from him.

Having a Child

Sitting with the elders, memories from my youth returned to me. The old people of the tribe would watch young people and when the children began changing their conduct, attitude, and behavior the elders would recognize that they were turning into young men and women. The old men of the tribe would begin to teach a young lad the spiritual protocol at ceremonies and how to behave as a man and not a boy. Now he would have to begin taking more responsibility in the tribe and most important he would be taught about his responsibility to protect and respect all women. Especially women who were not alone (pregnant). Only when a man has learned to live in peace and harmony can he lay with someone and have the honour to raise one of Creator's children.

It was also a very special time for a young girl when she goes into her woman time (first menstruation.) The old women of the tribe would have the responsibility of teaching a young girl about her upcoming womanhood. They would go to her each with a message. These messages were all about proper behavior for a woman. Especially when she was in her 'moon' time (when she was menstruating) also called her 'power' time. The old ones would talk about all the gifts and responsibilities of being a woman. Most important of all was her gift to bring another little human into this world.

The moon time was a time to take especially good care of herself. She was not to allow herself to get cold and shiver. Never have intercourse in her moon time even after she married. After marriage a man and woman would not even sleep in the same place at that time. Everyone knew that a woman was so powerful that she was to stay away from all medicine bundles or sacred ceremonies. She also had to stay away from elders as she could overpower them at that time. Some tribes built a special lodge for her. Staying away from the sweat lodges, the sun dances and the pipe was also a must. A young woman knew the protocol and respected it. Now she was powerful enough to create another little human being. It was a very sacred time for her to take care of herself. Everyone had a special respect for her at that time. Young women were taught the beauty ways. Even to this day, they carry our greatest hope for the future. Those who know this will always honour and protect them.

The coming together of a young man and a young woman did not take place until they were ready, usually by their mid-twenties. We used to have only small families. Mostly one or two children. We were taught to keep our population low, so that we could devote all the time needed to each child. We had birth control. The prospective mothers were given herbs to take if the time was not right to have a child. Another herb would reverse the effects if they decided to bring another little being into this world. Only when a couple got the message that the time was right would they have a child. When an egg was fertilized in a woman and a little being began to grow it was such a sacred time for the mother and the community. It was important for the mother to be in balance and harmony when she was carrying her child and everyone in the community were very mindful and respectful. The old teachings were that whatever the mother experiences are taken on by the little being, who would be affected in body, mind, heart, and spirit within the womb. With this understanding, the enlightened ones knew that they were teaching the unborn babies as they taught the mothers.

When that little being made its appearance, the old women would drum that new little life into this world. That way they would always connect to the beat of the drum, the heartbeat of Mother Earth. All the men and children were not allowed to come too close, but we would listen for that drumbeat, and we would know the baby had made its appearance. Everyone would celebrate the appearance of the gift from the Creator.

Raising a Child

When I was born, everyone including my parents, the grandparents and the whole village became teachers to me. Everyone shared their particular talents as soon as I was old enough. The responsibility of teaching lay with all tribal members.

So as children we grew up feeling precious as the community recognized us for our innocence and our wisdom. We would never be scolded, but when we needed a teaching, we would be given one, mostly from one of the elders. Sometimes the teachings would be harder than punishment.

As the elders and the children are closest to the Creator, we understood each other. For generations our people were very conscientious about the responsibility of spiritual teachings of a child, so the child can stay in the intuitive and nurture the instincts one is born with. As the children grew, the parents and grandparents took care that the child was taught what it needed to know to sustain itself in later life. The old ones understood that punishment had no place in the life of a child. It would injure their spirit.

I remember freely running and playing with my brothers and sisters. I remember being told how rich we were because we had game, fish, wild berries, and vegetables. We would pretend that we were great hunters. We liked to make spears and bows and arrows and then try to be as accurate as possible in hitting a small tree. One thing about our games, they were not competitive with each other. We would just try to do better ourselves and when we did everyone cheered. My favorite time of the year was the fall. I loved the sound of the dried leaves as we ran and played.

There was an abundance of saskatoons, raspberries, strawberries, pin cherries and cranberries. They would be in different places and ripen at different times, so we would move to where the berries were and pick whatever we needed for the winter. Racks were built where the berries could be dried so they would keep until they were used. I remember how I loved the soup with berries in it that my mother made all through the winter.

I do not remember ever being scolded by anyone. I remember one time in particular when my friends and I followed the old men to a special place. We hid in the bushes and watched them. First, they scraped off the top layer of soil including the grass. Underneath was some red dirt that the men began rolling around in. They even ate some; all the while talking about how this dirt was so good for healing. I think I might be able to find that place today. So much has changed that I am not certain.

The older boys did not want us young ones around, but we followed anyway. We so wanted to learn how to snare rabbits and birds from the trees, just like they did, and to catch geese and ducks who had landed in the water. They held their breath, dived down under the bird and pulled the birds under water and drowned them. There was supper! Sometimes the young men would almost drown themselves in the hunt, sputtering and coughing. One time one of the guys got under the geese and grabbed two. Those geese just dragged him along in the water. We all stood on the shore and laughed and laughed. This is mostly how I grew up my first six years of life. After that all hell broke loose.

Burial Rites

In the days of my youth, I remember my mother and other community members making preparations for the end of someone's earth journey, to once again return to the spirit world from which they came. Family and friends would journey far to gather together to support the person transitioning. All would gather in fellowship and prayer for a good journey. When an elder passed over, everyone was aware of the wisdom being lost to the people left behind. We would say that when an elder left we lost a whole library of knowledge.

Once a person left, and we were all gathered the elders would once again lead everyone in prayer. Everyone would share about how the departed had lived, especially funny experiences they may have had together. It was against protocol to talk about how one died.

The remains would be wrapped in hides and then laid on a platform, which the young men built. Some tribes hung the body of their loved ones in a tree. Again, each tribe was just a little different, so I can't say everyone did things in that exact way, but everything was always done with very sacred ceremonies. The drummers would drum their spirit on their way all the while singing the sacred songs. One year after the passing there would be a special ceremony performed by the elders of our tribe. Four pipes would be smoked. More ceremonies would be held each year, with one pipe being removed each time. Altogether there would be four memorials. Some tribes kept a little bit of the hair and put it in a sacred bundle only to be opened in the fall when the memorial tea dances were held. Some did not.

It was hard for my people when the Euro/Canadians brought us new laws. We were forced to bury our dead in the ground. If we did not the consequences would be jail. That was one of the changes that was most difficult for my ancestors. My people believed that putting the remains up high would facilitate an easier journey to the spirit world. Switching to burials was difficult indeed. We had to make changes so new traditions were brought to us. Elders would have visions about it. When we did farewell ceremonies, we covered the graves with a tiny dwelling. They were reminders that the departed had gone home. They kept the memory of the deceased person alive for the people who were left behind. It was a reminder of their physical earth journey.

Governance

Our community had our own system of government. The wisest, bravest, and strongest would govern along with our visionaries, teachers, healers, and others. Each family would appoint their best to be their representative on council. Although there was a headman, there would be hours of discussion with their families as to what the best decision would be for the people. When council was held, all members of the tribe could attend. Every decision was made by consensus. There was no overpowering of one another as everyone was given the right to speak. Adjustments were constantly made with each contribution. Every decision took as long as it took to come to consensus.

After consensus was reached, the camp crier, who was the village announcer for all the news, would go around the community, loudly calling out the outcome. A camp criers had to be very eloquent speakers who could relate council's decisions in a concise well-spoken manner.

Every time a headman was to be replaced; he would decide that it was time to pass that honour to someone else. He would present protocol to an oskapew (helper) who would then stay with him and take care of the headman. The headman would in turn teach the helper until he would have enough knowledge to take over. Although it was mostly men who were appointed as spokespeople, no decisions were ever made without consultation with the women. The women held the real power while the men were the spokespeople.

We did have some problems, but we had our ways of solving them too. My people had their ways of handling issues that caused disharmony amongst us. Disharmony could relate to a theft, infidelity, bullying, jealousy, or any number of issues which do occur in any community. There was no labelling of what might be civil or what might be criminal. The only criteria for anyone to face the community for correction was the fact that there was disharmony and harmony needed to be restored. There were no jails, no punishment, only teachings. Some lessons were difficult to learn. Standing in front of your whole community and speaking your truth and hearing other's truth was sometimes painful, but necessary in order to get to the truth and find solutions so harmony could be recreated. Take, for example, if one man killed another, even if it was accidental and he had much remorse for what he did, the community may order him to support the victim's family. He in turn would likely consider that fair as his actions did cause great loss whether he meant to or not.

In the case of infidelity, the injured couples would have to listen to the consequences of their actions, and everyone affected would speak. If no resolution was possible then banishment may be the end solution.

Bullying was another problem that came up off and on. Again, there would be a meeting of the community to try to resolve this problem. Each individual would share their feelings. The people who bullied would also have to explain why they bullied. Maybe there was a pain in the individual's life which needed attention. Maybe the person that was bullied was doing something to hurt the other person without even knowing what it was until they were brought before the community. When each party heard each other's truth and understood the consequences of their actions the problem was most often resolved just through understanding. In any case the problem must be resolved; banishment would be the very last resort. When a party is banished, they lose all contact with anyone from the tribe, even their families will not have contact. This was not done lightly.

Sometimes, when a rivalry between two men got out of hand, the elders would bring both together and make them sing a battle song to one another. They would face each other, some distance apart. The battle songs began with 'I'm going to go and die today.' When they really listened, they would soon realize they were singing the same song. The wind would go out of their sails and that was the end of that.

Hunting

The hunter would purify himself and his hunting gear and pray that only the animals that were willing to give their lives show themselves. He would also give thanks in advance for the gift they would receive. He would make a quick kill and approach the remains with quiet respect to the animal who had sacrificed itself. He would give thanks for a life given so he and his family could eat and survive.

The old ones talked about the fact that those who did not hunt with respect and proper protocol as they were taught would be heard for miles by the game and the animals would not show themselves to such a human. It was said that the elder could hear the cry of small voices under their feet. "This one has violated the universal and natural order of all life and the connection of those laws to Mother Earth and our Creator," the elders would say.

The taking of an animal for food had very specific ways of preparation in respect for the animal and the connectedness with all things. When you start cutting and opening an animal, the top correlates with the winter, the start of the yearly cycle. The ribs and internal right and left organs correlate the life that is given to us, for which we give thanks. As we further open the cycle correlation continues into the spring cycle to the summer and fall, and we are grateful for all the medicine of the animal. With respect and use of the four sections, we used to be healthy.

All parts are important as are all seasons. It is all in the university of life. It is a celebration of life. It is our expression of it. Everyone, including the animals, is connected to the Creator, so whatever we do not use goes back and nurtures the land. It all fits. There are those who know these things. There is much more to taking an animal than food.

Story tellers loved to tell hunting stories. They shared through stories how the natural law given to man gave him voice to ask permission from his relatives – the bear, the moose, the deer, and the buffalo – to give up their life, so that the human and his relations could eat and live, or how sometimes the animals would get the best of the humans. If they did not want to sacrifice themselves, they might turn on the human and chase them away. It was like a game.

Sometimes when one of the men would shoot a moose, the men would all help haul it to our village and everyone would help to cut up the meat and dry it for the winter, all the while thanking the Creator and the animal for the abundance. Sometimes the women would sing quietly while they worked. The hides would be stretched, and smoke-tanned. That was a big job as they were stretched on a home-made frame. The brain of the moose was used to soften the hide as it was scraped with a bone shaped just right for the task. Then a fire using willow trees would be built under the hide to help dry it out. It was a lot of work, but there were many hands to help. I remember everyone laughing and joking around, grateful for getting such a prized hide.

Fall equinox was a special time to give thanks for the berries and wild vegetables that were harvested and the meat that was prepared for the long winter months. I remember all our relatives getting together.

Tea Dances and Ceremony

Our tea dances were a very popular way for the community to celebrate together. While the drums were beating, and the songs were sung, and the people were dancing, the moss bag babies were either on their mothers' backs or were tucked safely away close to their family members.

At a tea dance four tipis make one long tipi and inside we have four little fires in a row. We have food on one side, and medicines on the other side. My grandfather used to do prayers at the tea dance ceremonies. When he did these, people made the claim that their ancestors actually came and gave them a hug, and they could feel that. I don't know of anyone who can do that today. We had singers and ceremonial people. Women sat to the left and the men to the right of the elders who sat at the front.

You lift the pipe before you do anything, and you move it in all the four directions. Then you move it above and you move it below, all the while praying. You bless the food and then you feed the flame with the food. When that part is done, now you can dance, and the drums start. Some may dance like a figure eight. You may dance with the fire itself or with anybody. You just get in there like a dirty shirt!

Because the Lubicon band never signed a treaty, we were not forbidden by law to do our ceremonies, but we were still harassed. Our little community would celebrate each part of this yearly cycle with ceremonies and giving thanks to Creator and the star people for passing the knowledge of these natural cycles. I was taught how to celebrate every season and every cycle in many ways. Pipoon (winter solstice) is the start of a new cycle. It is time for movement toward sekwan, (spring) and then to continue the cycle into nepon (summer) and again into takwaginor pipoon (fall) and then back to Pipoon, (winter solstice)

Gatherings and dances would take place for many occasions. Any excuse to have a gathering! Young men would be chosen to pass the message from village to village or the word would pass from one community to another by the visitors. The messengers would simply point at where the sun would be in the sky for time of day, and the moon phase to know which day. The moccasin telegraph worked well, and everyone knew where and when to meet. Families would put up these dances to acknowledge those still on their earth walk and commemorate and honor those who were departed. Nature and the seasons would also be honored in a combination of the physical and the mystical world. Certain dances can only be done at the appropriate time of the year.

Sometimes a man would be honored with the presentation of an eagle feather. Traditionally women were not given feathers but would be publicly presented with a special gift such as a buckskin dress, a special headband, or a special pair of moccasins. These special presentations were a big honor and served to keep our tribes strong and of good character overall.

Certain ceremonies, like pipe ceremonies, were not to be attended by children. The spirits were called to give guidance to the elders. As children are too pure, and they might decide to follow the spirits into the spirit world when they left after the ceremony was complete. I was always so curious, and I would sneak a peek whenever I had a chance. One time I got caught by an elder who gave me 'the look' and I scurried away.

I do remember we had ceremonies which were meant as teachings and the feast of the maidens was one of those. If, for instance, one maiden may have talked badly about another. They would then sit together with an old lady and talk until the truth came out. No one could fool an old lady. The maiden who was the target would be asked to put on a feast to clear her name. If she did not do so, it would mean that she was guilty of whatever she was accused of. No such feast could be held without truth. I do have vague memories of this, but it was only when I was older that I fully understood the purpose of the feast.

There was a special ceremony when a couple separated: a blanket would be split in public. The elders would have a long talk with both parties about the consequences of the split. Especially where children were involved. The elders would emphasize the consequences to all the loved ones and how they still had responsibility as a mother or father. It was a big shame, as the process was so public, and everyone would know that they could not get along.

The 'black robes,' like shadows in the trees, were coming for us. They and the 'yellow stripes' began sneaking around and listening. One time a big shot priest came with lots of people, and they destroyed our pipes and our drums and family bundles and all the sacred things we had. Our little village was devastated. For our small community who had never before been invaded it was hard to understand why anyone would do such a thing. After that the yellow stripes would walk around outside the tipis, and would listen for drums. If they heard drums they would come in and they would confiscate everything, the drums, the pipes, everything!

The newcomers needed to do away with all that Indian culture. Then we started to do the ceremony without the drums, and we would just beat the tipi pole, very lightly, so outsiders would not hear.

We all had to be very secretive about where the tea dances were held, as people were put in jail at that time for their dance. Everyone was careful where and to whom they made the announcement of their celebrations. We were taught not to talk to just anyone about where and when we met up. Smoke signals and the moccasin telegraph, news brought from person to person, was alive and well. Our sweat lodges now had to be moved far into the bush to not be discovered because if the wrong people found us, our family members would be arrested and put in jail. There was also resistance from within our own community, from 'born again Christians' who also fought the traditional ways and were quick to notify the authorities when traditional gatherings were held.

It was like everyone seemed to be fighting for people's souls. In our traditional way, people were free to choose. We were encouraged to be free thinkers. Hell, and damnation were not in our world.

We had heard that the government was going to come one day and take us away from our families. That they wanted to take the Indian out of the Indian. They wanted to make us just like the white man. As our only experience was with the traders, and that was not bad, we did not really appreciate what that meant. My mother did see the advantage of learning a new language and the white man's way of working with numbers and she prepared me with the fact that I would learn things that would help me in this new life we were all facing.

Part 2
Residential School

Village suffering

There were many changes to come for everyone. When the residential school was set up in Grouard in 1939, the yellow stripes and black robes invaded every community, including ours, and took all the school age children away. It was just a terrible time for everyone. We did not have serious diseases like TB at that time and if someone got sick our medicine people knew how to make them better. Once the children were taken away, our families never knew if they would ever come back. Too many never did. Our communities never knew who would come home until July of every year when the kids who had survived would return. Then we would have ceremonies for the lost children. All the people would gather in their grief. After all every child was considered as belonging to everyone in the community.

The children died of the white man's sickness. Some were taken in the middle of the night and never came back. Sometimes us boys were woken up and told to dig a grave. We all knew where the grave sites were. We were afraid they were killed by those horrible human beings. We did not know those kinds of people existed. Looking back, I can now more than ever before appreciate the richness of what the Creator gave us, of the happiness of my people before contact.

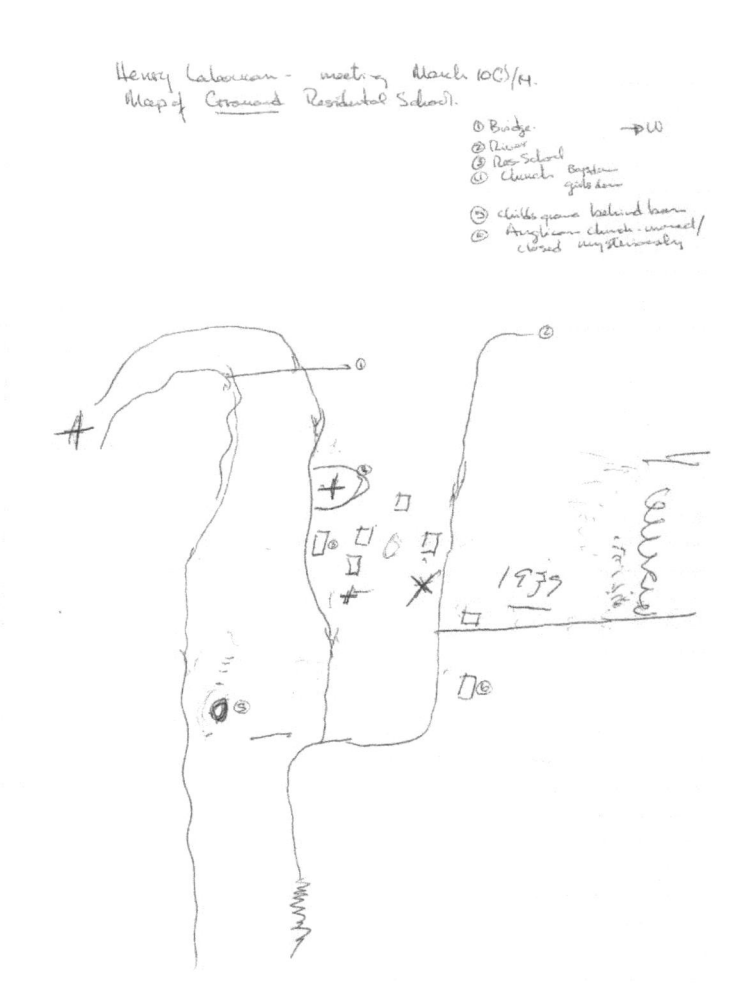

Map of the Grouard residential school including the children's graveyard.
By Henry

Those who did return were 'different'. They were no longer the happy little beings they were. Many became silent and withdrawn. No one understood what happened as the children could not put words to the horror they lived. They could not find the words to explain it in the Cree language so most kept all that pain inside and it was only with the introduction of the Truth and Reconciliation Commission, which was established in 2008, that many put words to that torture. Even their own children and grandchildren never heard what really happened in those schools before. It has been so hard on my people. I saw what happened to my brothers after they went to the white man's school. They were no longer happy like they were before, so I knew I would not be going to a good place. My biggest shock was when I saw my brothers with short hair. They looked just so awful. My brothers did teach me some English and they told me that I could no longer speak my old language in school, that from now on I would have to only speak a new language. It would be much easier for me in school if I learned the white man's language before I went. I was called by my second name, Henry all the time after that. I was so afraid when I thought about what was going to happen to me, so I tried not to think about it.

The kidnapping

My mother tried her best to prepare me even if I did not understand why at the time. I don't know how much my mother knew about the details of what happened. She told me that if anyone ever made me uncomfortable, no matter who they were I was to holler "Kaya! Kaya!" as loud as I possibly could and then run for the nearest door. Try to make sure there were other people around at all times. She told me to learn the white man's reading and writing because it would be good to know these things when I was a man. She too was a seer, just like my grandfather.

In the old days all clothing was made of moose, deer or buffalo hides. In school no one was allowed to wear that, so my mother got 'white' things for us three boys by preparing furs and trading at the Bay. She did all she could to make our lives as easy as possible. Still, she could not protect us from the hell to come. She tried her best to learn this new language. She did see the benefit in that.

One day it happened. I will never forget how the yellow stripes barged right into our home and pulled me away from my mother who was hanging onto me for dear life. I didn't want to leave our home and she did not want me to go. She just cried and cried when the yellow stripes pulled me out of her arms. I had never heard my mother cry before and that made me cry too. She was just not strong enough to hold me, so I was thrown in the back of a wagon with the rest of the kids from our village. We knew from others who had made that trip before us that it would take three or four sleeps. One man was on a horse and following along to make sure no one ran away.

These horse men were native guys who worked for the school. The school and the Bay were the only sources for cash so they did what they thought they had to do to feed their families.

I was so angry for what those horsemen did that I decided to try to sneak off and run back home. No luck! I got caught and was thrown back in the wagon. I ran away again and got caught again. That was when the guy on the horse tied me up and put me in front of the saddle on his horse like a dead animal or something. He just kept me tied up all the way. Never had I been tied up before. In fact, I was always a free spirit up until then. This was just a nightmare.

The Arrival to Torture

When we arrived I saw these huge buildings. The biggest one I had ever seen before was the Bay trading post. I had never seen brick before. It all looked so scary and I was just a little guy. The scariest of all was when I saw this big sword on top of a building. I knew then that I was going to die in this awful place.

When the wagon stopped there was a whole row of black robes, and some were women. They all had little swords in their waist bands and those swords were right at my eye level. That was the most fearful moment of all, and I looked around to see if I could escape, but the man on the horse was watching me, so I just followed the others into what I knew was hell.

The first thing that happened was that we were lined up and everyone got their hair cut. My hair was slightly curly, and I was so proud of it. People always said something nice about my hair. I was in shock to see it falling to the floor. I thought I was going to die right then and there. Then we were stripped down given a shower. That too was horrifying. No one had ever seen me naked that I could remember. We were always modest. The nuns and priests washed what was left of our hair with a terrible smelling stuff which I later learned was kerosine. Just in case we had bugs my brothers had told me. By this time, we were tired and hungry. We were all led to a room with long tables and chairs. The nun brought us each a bowl of porridge. And then we were marched to another room.

There we saw a room full of white metal beds with white bedding. They were only about two feet apart and there were so many. We were each assigned a bed with a number on it. That number would follow us all through school.

The next day we were woken up early and told to wash up make our beds and all stand at attention until we were ordered to march down to the dining room where we were once again fed porridge. I sure learned to hate porridge. Then it was off to the classrooms. Then we had to stand up and bow our heads. One of the boys didn't bow enough so the nun came with a big stick and hit him. I bowed deeper. I didn't want to get hit too. After they told us all about their Jesus and their God, the nun put some chicken scratches on the board. They meant nothing to me, so I just called them chicken scratches. That went on for about an hour or so and then it was time for lunch which generally consisted of some watered-down soup with a little meat and veggies that were all new to me. Not like the ones from home that we picked wild. So, soups bread and porridge were our main meals. In the afternoon the girls went to work cooking and cleaning. They baked all our bread. They also washed all the floors and the dishes, so they were kept busy until suppertime. Us boys did get to go outside, but that was just so we could work in the garden and look after the animals which provided all our food. With only so little classroom time it was no wonder we only had about a grade two level of education. Many were still totally illiterate when they left school at age sixteen. For sure not prepared to live in the newcomers' world and also not at ease on the reserves after the brainwashing everyone got about hell. The way I look at it is that the hell is right here on earth. Not in the spirit world.

We were not allowed to look at the faces of any of the white people. We had to look down in their presence. We were just not fit to look at their faces, but that was ok as there was nothing good to see there anyway. Except for one nun. She was so kind and tried to comfort us any time she found someone crying. She was our only comfort. She would even play games with us and sometimes she would laugh out loud, and we knew she was a good person. She and another priest, Father Van der Stein were real good people. Father Van Der Stein even learned to speak Cree as soon as he could. My mother spoke often of him and how her father took him as his brother. Father Van der Stein was a bush man and a hunter, and he would never hurt a child. He was even given one of the highest honours anyone can receive from the Native people, a traditional name. We called him Muskwa, Black Bear. I think he and the other nun kept many of us alive. One day she just disappeared, and no one spoke her name again.

Muskwa was not pleased with the school's attitude, as the mission was to take the 'Indian out of the Indian' and Father Van der Stein was, for sure, not doing a good job of that. Instead, he became immersed in our community, learning from our elders. When he became a Bishop, he continued to fight hard for the rights of my people.

One day a big-shot priest came to our village. I don't know where he came from, but he had lots of people with him – 'black robes' and 'yellow stripes' – that was how I knew that he must be some kind of big shot. He ordered the destruction of all the sacred things in our community. They broke the pipes, took the bundles and destroyed all the ceremonial things they could find. The next morning a sacred pipe was found in pieces. It was devastating for us. Father Van der Stein heard about the incident and hurried to the village. He helped us pick up every piece of the pipe and put it back together. It was actually smoked again. I have seen that pipe.

The other nuns and priests just told us that we would never amount to anything. We would be nothing but dirty Indians. Our parents and grandparents were that too and they did everything they could to make us believe that. We were told that we would go to hell, and so would all our relatives if we did not change our ways. There would be no place for us or our family in heaven. We felt so much fear for going to hell, and we feared for our parents and grandparents as well. These were new concepts for us. We knew of a wonderful place for everyone in the spirit world after we left this earth. We knew nothing about heaven and hell. All this was so confusing for a child. I have to admit that they made me feel ashamed of my bloodline. That is a terrible thing to do to a child. I never knew anger before, now I had anger. I didn't understand what I was angry about. I was just angry.

On the wall in our classroom and in every room at the school there were large posters. They were developed by Father Lacombe in 1864 who was given the task of opening schools for the Cree and the Blackfoot in Canada. This poster was printed at the University of Ottawa and was used as a teaching tool to explain our destiny as ordered by God. It demonstrated the chaos on earth before the birth of Christ and how all that changed with his teachings. If you were born white, you would go straight to heaven as was demonstrated by a yellow path on the left side of the poster. It led directly to a picture of a blonde girl in the arms of Jesus, surrounded by angels.

On the right side of the poster there was a dark pathway which, if followed, would lead straight to hell with no opportunity of ever making it to heaven. The Native way was on that pathway as were all people of color, all black people too. However, colored people could also come to heaven, if we crossed over and changed to a yellow pathway and became Catholic. There would be some delay though, as people with color would still burn in purgatory for a while before entering heaven. As I lay in my bed, I could always see the posters. There were five in our big room.

I had never been told about hell or heaven before. I had learned that when people die they transition from their earth walk to the spirit world. Now I was alone and scared of hell. We just knew we did not want to go to hell, and so many of my people converted.

I would watch and see what made the nuns and the priests happy. When certain words were used that made them happy, so I tried to copy those words. Certain chicken scratches made them happy, so I did my very best to copy those too.

The worst thing happened when this one nun got dirty with me. I can't say any more. You are too good of a friend, and I can't talk about these things to someone I really care about, but I can tell you I had no use for white women after that. It took many years for me to get over that. After that I tried to stay in the classroom as much as possible and I studied real hard and got way ahead. I was too afraid to be caught alone with any nun.

The first time I went to confession and told the priest what happened with the nun he was so angry and told me not to lie in confession. Bad choice on my part. They punished me for the littlest things after that.

It didn't take us long to figure out what the priest wanted to hear, and we turned confession into a big joke. They would start to breathe really fast if we told them about having sexual thoughts and feelings toward the girls, so we confessed to all kinds of things like how we would look under their skirts. That would really get us some praise for our confession and never too harsh punishments.

I think the worst was the nights the priests walked between the rows of beds and picked a boy and took him away. They knew to pick on those too afraid to resist. Some never came back. The beatings were unbearable. We were always on guard for the black robes after dark when we were supposed to be sleeping. How we hated the black robes. Us boys used to talk about it when we had a chance. They would say that the priest put his, you know what, up their butts, and it hurt real bad. That is why so many could never marry and turned to alcohol and drugs. They could not ever go with a woman and have a healthy relationship.

Many died under the bridges or froze to death in the alley ways. Our people became so sick from what they experienced in residential school. Too many just gave up on life. This open preying on us by the pedophiles went on from back in the 1870s to the closing of the last residential school in 1996.

One thing I did enjoy was working with the animals until one day when I went to the barn and the guy who looked after the animals made indications that he was up to no good. I just screamed "Kaya!!" Kaya!!" as my mother taught me and ran as fast as I could out of that barn. I never went back in there again. Some boys were too afraid to scream, so those were the ones that were targeted. The abuse happened in every building, in every dark corner the pedophile nuns and priests could find. The abuse happened to both the boys and the girls. They even had a house for the girls who got pregnant. We boys, in our innocence just saw them as chubby and we thought they were teacher's pets because we thought that they were just well fed while we were starving. Of course we learned better when we got older. I often wondered what happened to those babies. I know sometimes people would come and take them away. I know now that some went to other countries. I wonder where our relatives are today. I wonder if they even know where they came from. The girls never talked about their giving birth again. It was a great secret, but I am sure they must have missed their babies even if the priests were the fathers. That was another truth that many first shared with the Truth and Reconciliation Commission. Even families learned about what happened for the first time. It has all been a burning secret in my people's hearts for so many years as they suffered in silence.

Those priests and nuns just did anything, just anywhere, any place, including the class room when they thought nobody was around. On the outside they were so holy, but inside there lived a monster. They punished us a lot for the littlest things. Even if we looked at their faces we would be punished. We were never safe from being hit. One day a nun took a stick and tried to hit me on my head, but I put up my hand to protect it. She actually broke my thumb and it has been disfigured ever since. Later I got an operation so I could actually use it again. I still have scars all over my back from being hit. They broke both my wrists when I tried to protect myself.

A horse strap or the big ruler was always in their hands in the classrooms. Anything that was handy. Many times we would go to bed without supper if we did something they didn't like.

Sometimes we were not allowed to watch the odd movie that was brought in. That devastated us.

Most of us had never seen a movie and that would be the highlight of the year.

Sometimes when someone peed the bed they would be made to stand in front of everyone with the wet sheet over their heads. Peeing the bed often happened and I think now it was because no one could ever relax in that hell we were living.

One of the most embarrassing things was when we needed to go to the bathroom and we had to raise our hands with either one or two fingers up according to our needs. Sometimes the nuns and the priests wouldn't give permission and some students peed themselves. Then they would embarrass them in front of the whole class. It was all we could do not to beat them up. That feeling was new to us too because we were always taught to respect women and then these women did that to the girls! The pain in our hearts was overwhelming. We did not know that such evil existed. Sometimes when I think about these things I cry. Even today. I have hearing aids now because I was hit so many times on the side of my head. It was just one bad day after another, but we figured out how to make the best of it. I actually learned how to leave my body and then they could do whatever they wanted and it didn't hurt, but sooner or later I would come back and the pain would come too. All the time we tried to do everything they wanted us to do so we would not get punished.

During the summer we did get to go back home, but I couldn't talk to anyone about the school. I just didn't have the words in my mother's and grandparents' language. I'm not sure I could have told anyway. It was just too painful. In the fall when we were picked up again everyone, our whole community, the old people, the parents, the children all were crying. The police were there to arrest anyone who tried to stop the children from going.

Later my mother did leave our community and bought a house close to the school. That way we could go home at night and life was much better. She continued to tell us stories every night. She took away all the awful stuff and we slept like a log after that.

I think we all survived because we sure knew how to tell good jokes and laugh at the darndest things. We really tried to find any little bit of fun we could. When they made us sing we used to change the words. We changed the words of one hymn to "Suffer the little children and bring them to me" when it should have been 'Suffer the little children to come onto me.' We would all laugh. They never caught on. We always said that we did not believe that Jesus would be like these evil people. I even said that, and I think that is why I was always getting hit.

I think the nuns and priests were not happy either as I saw the strain on their faces. I never heard them laugh and sometimes I even felt sorry that they were so unhappy. They all seemed to become afraid when I said, "would Jesus do that?" Then I would really get a beating on my poor little brown body. We learned what they liked, and we gave it to them. We really learned to lie at residential school. When we got older, the staff did become afraid of us and pretty much left us alone. One day we just knew that we had the power now.

One of the priests was worse than all the others. Father Tessier was his name, and he definitely had a black soul. One time when I was about 14 or 15 years old, I was blamed for something I didn't do, and he was going to make me pull my pants down and bend over and he was going to beat me on my naked butt in front of everyone.

Knocking Out the Priest

All at once all the rage of all those years welled up in me and I just hit him so hard that I knocked him out cold. Everyone just applauded in utter and complete joy. I turned on my heels and walked right out with my head held high. That was the big life changer for me. Just as I walked out from that school, I saw two familiar faces, Dan McLean and Dave Kappo drove by and I waved them down. Dan and Dave were clearing right-of-ways for power lines at Little Prairie, close to what is now Chetwyn, B.C.

I asked if I could get a job. They just laughed. I was much too small for such hard work. I told them I had just knocked out the Father Superior. They never said another word, just motioned for me to get in the back of their van and away we went.

I was on top of the world getting out of hell and knocking out the Father Superior. Woo hoo!!!

I was elated as I perched in the back of that old van. Now I had a job, I would be able to provide for my mother. I was free from the shackles of the residential school.

Part 3
The Raging Years

The further away from the school the better. Then I got too tired to think and I fell asleep. When we arrived in camp it was pitch dark. Dan pointed me to a cot in a tent and I just flaked.

The morning after he gave me a small Pioneer saw to use. "Just right for Henry" they said. We cut trees to make way so the power lines could be installed. I worked as hard as any man, and they paid me accordingly.

The good food was wonderful. That was one thing about camps. We were always well fed.

What happened next is hard for me to talk about. I had put many painful memories away. Telling you this, the pain is coming back. I know I need to do this so let's get on with it.

Everything was good on the outside, but on the inside, the pain of what happened all those years in school became all-consuming and an overwhelming rage I never knew I had welled up in my whole being. I couldn't get the picture of those dirty old priests feeling up the girls out of my head. I missed my friends. I had taken care of them and now I was not there to defend them. I could not stop thinking about my family and the abuse my siblings suffered either. I could not stop thinking about my mother's pain. I could not stop thinking.

The hard, physical work was not only good for my body, but was also good for my soul. At least it kept my mind occupied for some hours of the day and kept the rage under control, sort of. In the evenings the boys in the camp would laugh together, tell jokes together, but we all knew that underneath the surface we were all tormented by our common past. We had all been through hell at the schools. That made us brothers. I managed to get through the days, but the nights on my cot were pure torture. I would curl up and fold my arms over my heart. I was dead tired, so sleep would come quickly, but it was pure torture. I had nightmares every night.

Hatred

My hatred toward white people grew and grew. They had taken my brothers and sisters, they violated our beautiful young girls and boys. Peace and harmony were no more. Our elders' hearts were broken, my mother's heart was broken. All that was important and beautiful from my life before we were taken away was gone, and it was the white people's fault. How I hated them.

One day Dan and Dave told me they were moving camp to Hinton, Alberta. I panicked. I did not want to go back to Alberta. Even if the school was over 600 kilometers away, I hated being even that close. I was living under a shadow. I knew if the RCMP ever caught up with me I would be in big trouble. I didn't want to go, but in the end, I decided to. I had people who cared about me in camp, and I guess I needed that.

I think we survived the hell we were put through only because we know how to have fun. We made sports days with races and ball games, which gave us a bit of relief. However, if anyone crossed me, I took them down. I would beat on my poor victims relentlessly until someone pulled me off. I couldn't stop myself. I became tough, angry and raging. My little brown body became stronger, but the pain remained in my soul.

One day, I made myself brass knuckles by melting down the lead weights from fishing supplies. They made up for what I was missing in size. I was afraid of no one and welcomed any fights I could find, especially with white guys. It gave me great comfort to beat them up. I know it was not good and I am embarrassed about it now, but it was what it was. There was only one good thing to live for. I snuck home to see my mother occasionally to give her money.

Both my older brothers were on the drinking path, and they decided to move in with my mother. I hated it so much as she was hurting to see her sons turning to alcohol as so many did in those years. I told my mother to send them away. You sent your husband packing why do you not do that with your sons as well. I cannot support them in that lifestyle. I will continue to support you and my sisters, but I do not want any of my money used for booze. I did not want my mother to suffer any more. Eventually they left. I guess my mom gave them the boot.

Every time I left my mother's little cabin the rage would immediately return. I so wanted to stay longer and help her. I could not. The police would get me for sure.

My first six years after residential school I put four white guys in hospital, almost killing them. Rage was my driving force, so where is common sense!? It was not there. Once in a great while I went into town with my buddies, but that was always trouble. If some white guy even looked at me the wrong way, I would go eyeball to eyeball with him and ask why he looked at me like that. Before he could even answer, I would knock him down flat. Then it was into the old camp truck, and I spun the tires as I left in a cloud of dust. It felt so good, but I knew if I got caught, I would be in big trouble.

So much I loathed about this new life. I hated using our white names, which meant nothing, but if we wanted to travel, to work, or even to open a bank account we had to. That was just how it was. It was no wonder we raged. Some are still raging. We were forced into a world where we did not belong, our identity was taken from us, our peaceful life was gone.

One day I heard the McKenzie fisheries shut down at Faust on Lesser Slave Lake and moved to Hay River on Great Slave Lake. Some of my pals went with them and some decided to try the west coast. When I found out, I decided to go with my buddies to Prince Rupert. "Why not try my hand at fishing?" I thought. Maybe I could learn something new. I would be further from the school and now I could work with family. Everyone from the north was family whether we were related by blood or not. Our common experience in the residential school made us brothers, and we understood each other, including the torment we all harbored.

I got a job on a boat called White Creek. My job was as a lookout for jumping fish and as soon as I would spot the right ones the nets would go down. We always had the best catch, and it was with great pride we would chug into Port Edward where we would sell our fish to the cannery. We could take home up to 1,100 dollars in four days. That was good money back then.

Crazy Crees

Our group from the north developed a close comradery and was respected or feared by all. We made our mark. We were known as the Crazy Crees. We would take chances on the water that no one else would. We were violent as hell and white guys would not want to cross our paths. We just loved to take a round out of them. When I think of it now, I see how wrong we were, but at the time it gave us great satisfaction. I think the locals were jealous because we were taking their jobs.

Even under the circumstances we always kept our sense of humour with our pals. One day we were all down at the wharf when a woman came walking by. The fellows were all looking her over when suddenly she fell, and her skirt went flying up, exposing much more than she had wanted. She was so embarrassed as all of us young fellows laughed so hard. I was embarrassed for her but didn't want to let on in front of the guys. Some ran over immediately to appear helpful, but they had another agenda. They were all laughing like hell as they tried to pick her up. One of our fellows told the others to lay off. "She's my sister and I will take care of her!" No one wanted to fool around with a pal's sister, so they left her alone. Later we found out she was not his sister at all, but he wanted her for his girlfriend.

We all goofed around a lot those days. One day Danny, one of the fellows on our crew fell off the dock. He screamed louder and louder and we laughed louder and louder. We thought he was goofing around. "I can't swim!" he kept hollering, but we didn't believe him. Suddenly I realized he really was in trouble, and I grabbed a big hook we used on the boats, and I threw it to him and we pulled him out. We laughed until we were almost hysterical. Danny was not impressed. He almost drowned and he was angry. That made it even more funny. It was our sense of humour that kept us going in those years. It still is. Without that we would simply die. Even if we laughed at each other, we were still a team. There was a special bond between us.

In 1956 I went back to the bush and took a job cutting right-of ways for laying pipelines. I felt safer from myself in the bush. The surveyors came first, staked out the exact place the pipeline would be placed. They put little stakes in the ground where it would be laid. When they had completed their work, the heavy equipment moved in and dug the trenches for the pipeline. Railway ties were laid in the bottom to support the pipes and prevent too much sinking. Big trucks brought the pipe as close as they could, and the rest was hauling the equipment especially designed for that purpose. After the preparation was completed, the pipe would be laid in the trenches. A primer was applied. Then we took off the excess, using big brushes in preparation for welders. It was all done by hand. That was my job.

After the weld, rubber aid was wrapped around for a better seal. I made good money there and enjoyed working in the bush, but still the fire burned in my gut, and I couldn't get the abuse out of my mind. Especially the dirty priests molesting our girls. The one thought that did put a smile on my face was when I would picture Father Superior go down.

When the project came to an end, I went back to Hinton to work with my old bosses again. That was the year I bought my first car. It was a 1949 Ford with a V8 engine. I went to a car dealership in Edmonton and paid cash up front. I was ready to go. In order to get a driver's license, you simply went to the RCMP, who took you for a short drive. You paid 50 cents and you got your license. That would have been so easy, if I had not been a wanted man in Alberta after knocking that priest out. If the police found me, they would immediately throw me in jail. So, no driver's license for me. I was so proud of my new car, but the fact that I couldn't get a driver's license made me even more angry.

Racism was so bad in those days and lots of us were thrown in jail whether we were guilty or not. Often, we were. I couldn't chance any contact with the law, but if anyone made any racist remark, my brass knuckles would come out and the fight was on. No wonder we were always running from the cops.

After that I travelled here and there and did different jobs including picking sugar beets outside of Taber and Lethbridge Alberta. We young people worked hard. Sometimes white women would chase me, but I stayed away from them.

I did not want to have anything to do with white people. Not even the women. In fact, my buddies who did take these women up on their flirting ended up in trouble. Not that I was afraid of trouble. Those women were just not for me.

I loved my car and drove with my head held high. This was mine; I had worked hard for it and, except for my clothes and my brass knuckles, it was my only possession. I was young, proud foolish and raging. I took my new car to drive home to my mother to give her some money, and as I drove through Grouard I saw the residential school. I took a turn and drove in on the school yard and spun lots of huies in that yard. I just spun around and around. I was good for nothing, a useless Indian, and see me now, I have a car! I made it without them. This young man was not a loser. I was one proud dude that day. I will never forget it.

One day me and buddies were driving around, and we saw a bunch of white guys. One of my buddies shouted, "Hey, you whities are nothing but fags!" They turned and shouted back "Hey, you useless good-for-nothing savages, you want to fight?" That was it. The fight was on. There was only three of us, and they not only outnumbered us, but they were much bigger too. We ran for my car as fast as we could, jumped in and locked the door. They continued to holler at us, and we hollered back. Eventually they turned and left. By this time, I was in a rage, and I decided not to let them get away with it. On went my brass knuckles. Out of the car I jumped and tore after these white trash guys. I caught one, grabbed that bastard and with one punch put him down. Then I turned to the next one. Down he went falling like a sack of potatoes. The others saw that and without looking back, ran away. When I turned to go back my chicken shit companions had stayed in the car. I couldn't believe they had not backed me up. I jumped back in the car and took off, wheels spinning. If we got caught, we would be in trouble for sure. No native person could win in a court of law.

The circuit judges travelled from community to community setting up court wherever the communities could facilitate it. We used to call the circuit judge in our area the 27-dollar judge. We called him that because any time any Native person appeared in front of him, he would immediately get a 27-dollar fine or jail time. Many didn't have the 27 dollars, so it was off to jail for them too. He hated us and we hated him. We were told to leave the court room without any chance to tell our story. We were summarily escorted out and taken to jail by the police. He took our freedom. That made us rage.

I liked my vehicle so much but trusted nobody. I would cut the wires underneath whenever I stopped so no one could steal it. When I was ready to go, I would get underneath and hook them up again and away I would go.

Every time I went home to my mother, she would remind me that the anger I carried would do me no good. If I did not deal with it, I would end up hurting or killing someone and going to jail for life. My mother had a sixth sense about that. I never told her. I knew she was right, but I wasn't ready. I saw her pain for the loss of her family to alcohol. I saw her fear for me.

"Your anger is hurting your own spirit," she would say." No one else's." I know now how much she must have suffered. I just thought that if I didn't drink, she would be ok, and I did not drink. But she was not okay. She knew my agony and it pained her.

As soon as I was of age, trouble found me. By this time, I was braver coming home as four years had passed since the incident with the priest, and I thought it was safe. I was wrong on that one. The police must have known I had turned eighteen and one day they were waiting for me when I arrived at my mother's place.

They put me in handcuffs, and I was arrested on the spot in front of my mother and sisters.

I was hauled in front of the circuit judge in Peace River and read out my charges. "You are charged with assault against the Father Superior of the Grouard residential school. How do you plead: guilty or not guilty? "I did take him down your honour, but he was coming at night and taking my friends. He was insulting and feeling up the young girls and I could not stand it any longer. It was too much, so I hit him so hard he went down with one punch. That was four years ago. Now I support my mother and sisters and work hard." Down came the gavel: "Three months in jail. Next. 'Justice' was fast and furious in those days.

As I sat in my cell, I had a lot of time to think. My worst nightmare was the fact that now my mother and sisters had no source of income. When I thought about that, all my hatred toward the whites boiled up inside me. They had taken me from my mother, had abused me at school, and now they had taken my freedom. It was all wrong. White faces were mean. I was filled with hatred for every one of them. I knew it was wrong. The elders had taught me to be better. I tried to make the anger stop but could not. It was a hard time, not being able to find our way in the traditional world and not belonging to any other world either. Even our identity was not acceptable.

When I left that jail, I headed to Moccasin Flats in Peace River. There was always boozing and fighting going on there. I went looking for my mother's husband, Albut. Couldn't say "my father." One day I ran into him and went face to face with him. All my anger and pain welled up and I took him by the scruff of the neck and stood him up against the wall. "You hurt my mother, you shot me, you did not care for anyone," I shouted at him without fear. I was ready to wipe him out. "I am no longer a boy," I shouted, "now I am a man!" When I saw the fear in his eyes I just dropped him and walked away. It felt good to have stood up to him and won.

After that I just wandered here and there doing whatever I could to bring money home, but I was never satisfied. It was never enough. The fire in my belly and the pain in my heart lived on.

I would drop in unannounced on any Native people whenever I felt like it. We had our ways. I was always welcome. They would just serve tea and whatever food they had. No questions asked.

With so many of us so angry and violent it was no wonder we had a bad reputation. Lots of my friends were in jail. Few really cared what happened to them. There was pain and drunkenness on the reservations. There was no peace anymore. Those who capitulated to the European way of life, were called apples. Red on the outside, white on the inside. One of the worst insults. Their money God mentality did not impress us. I felt helpless to change it, so I just carried on from one day to the next.

Bunky Willier

One time I will never forget was when my friend Bunky Willier was going out with a girl who had a cousin in Driftpile. He wanted to go and see her, so we jumped in my truck and drove over there. A bunch of guys from three families, seventeen in all, surrounded my truck and blocked our way.

They were shouting for us to get out. We were not budging. We locked the truck doors. Then they tried to break our windows with this big branch, so I just opened the door. They pulled Bunky out of the truck and beat him real bad.

I thought I could take down one or two anyway and I did. The rage took over I just kicked and kicked. When it was all over, they just left, and we were still alive. Bunky was such a comical guy. He looked at me and just laughed. "We got it, did we not?" His face was black and blue. Finally, the cops came. They took Bunky to the hospital. I didn't want to lay charges. I didn't trust the system, but Bunky insisted.

I waited till my strength was back a few months later and I did lots of pushups and exercises and horseback riding. I wanted to be mobile and flexible, you need to be able to duck quick. To only be strong doesn't help you. So, I trained to get strong enough and then I went to seek all these seventeen guys to give them a whipping. We'll see how tough they are if they meet me one on one.

The judge gave them a big lecture but surprisingly, no jail time. Only probation, with very strict rules. They were confined to their homes every night. After that Bunky and I stayed away from Driftpile. I was determined to get them all for hurting my friend and one by one I went after them.

The first one I found was Pha, which means "bad smell." I think he got his name only because his diaper as a child always smelled as his parents never took care of him.

I found Pha at a road construction site where they were re-doing a bumpy gravel road from Slave Lake to High Prairie. He was there driving a caterpillar to scrape the rough edges on the road.

When he saw me, he turned the machine around and tried to run over me, and suddenly his whole family was there, so of course I had to take off at that first time. After that incident with Pha and the caterpillar, I went after the rest of the guys, one by one by one. They knew I was coming for them.

The leader was Harry Govlay and I got Harry all by myself and knocked him flat with one blow. He got up and I knocked him down again, and again. But what hurt Harry Govlay the most is that I told him to crawl around his vehicle on his hands and knees. Can you believe it! Maybe I went too far with him. People were there watching.

The word was out after that, that I was dangerous. I did not care if I lived or died. I was not afraid of knives and guns. If I saw a guy with a gun, I walked up to him and challenged him. No one shot me. I'm not dead yet. I did get beat up a few times though, but I never stayed down. When I caught those guys off the reserve, I would challenge them to a fight, and they would be happy to take me on because I was not very big. I was like a raging bull and in a fair fight they could not beat me. The rage would take over. One by one I got them all.

One time I was having a soup lunch with my brother at my mother's house. He was one of those who never healed from the damage done to him. I was the main bread winner, and he was an alcoholic, and I told him so. His spirit was totally broken. I guess I should not have been talking to him like that, but I did, and the next thing I know, with no warning, he punched me real hard on my lower lip. It left a big hole, and my soup fell out of that hole. I stood up slowly taking a cigarette out of a package, lit it, and I put the cigarette in that hole, and I was smoking and blowing smoke from that hole, looking at my brother.

I think the incidents with Bunky and my brother began the change in me. I began to awaken to my mother's words when he came so close to death. I felt partly responsible. That hurt too. I did not want to be a part of losing my friends. I started to see that this life was getting me nowhere. Although I became aware it still took time before I seriously made a move for change.

I still got into fights time and again, but it gave me no pleasure. Sometimes when I walked away the fellows would call me a coward. I was too tired to care. I became aware that the white man would be here to stay. No amount of fighting on my part would change that.

My body was so affected by the rage that it prevented a healthy flow of body fluids, so it became sick. Nothing was in balance. Now I feel ashamed for what I did. I was so full of hurt and anger I didn't take the time to learn better. I was out of balance for some years, and I was not prepared to listen. I just wanted to stay in my negativity. I refused to let go. My pain and anger ruled me. I was not ruling myself. I was lost. I was living outside the laws of love. I knew it was time to turn to the old teachings of peace and harmony if I was to get better. We were forced to make the best of the reality of the invasion and the new way of life if we were to survive at all. My anger, resentment, hurt, and hate accomplished nothing. I almost lost my best friend. There was plenty to figure out. I became acutely aware of the waste of my life. I wanted to do better. I knew I had to do something to get myself under control. I could not take it out on my family. That was so against my mother's and her ancestors' teachings. I had seen the devastation alcohol had caused in too many community members and knew that was not an option for me.

I decided to go to Calgary to further my education. I had heard of Master Simon, a martial arts black belt teacher, who was in Calgary at the time. I decided to sign up for his course. I wanted to learn self-control. The course was extremely challenging, and two thirds dropped out before completion. I was not one of them. I began wandering to find my teachers. I guess I was ready.

I also thought about finding a wife and having a family. For the first time since residential school, I realized maybe I could have a good life again. For the first time I had hope.

Marriage

When I was in my mid-twenties and I began to realize that the nomadic life and the raging was not for me any longer, my thoughts wandered to settling down with a wife and starting a family. My mother was very strict about not even thinking that way until I prepared and could be stable enough to make a home and support that way of life. I saved my money from my work and purchased 18 acres of land in Grouard. Then I purchased a double wide trailer and parked it on that land. Now I was ready. One day I met my wife to be. I thought she would make a good mother for my children. After I turned 27, we married. I did have a boy and a girl.

Supporting all my family was of utmost importance to me so that meant I was away from home a lot. Soon things began to fall apart. My wife had become a devout Catholic, so when I went to the elders it really bothered her. She would call it the devil's work and was so angry. The fact that she was such a supporter of the church, which is based in fear, power and control, hurt my spirit. Her words reminded me of the nuns, and I would just cringe inside. How she could support the people who had hurt all of us so deeply, I could not understand. That was the way it was in those days. Families were torn apart, from the brainwashing that occurred in residential school which taught hatred, not love, they taught fear and division, not unity.

One time I came home and after a few days became very ill. I ended up near death. I felt that perhaps I would just leave this earth. But then suddenly I got a spiritual message that I had to go for help. I stumbled to my truck and drove myself to the hospital in High Prairie. I was so far out of it that I hit the ditch twice but managed to get back on the road and continued on. When I finally arrived, the doctor did not expect me to survive. I could not speak. The doctor decided to call in a priest to give me last rites. 'Coincidentally' Victor Prince, an elder, arrived at the hospital. When he entered my room and saw how ill I was he called his helpers and they called others. "Our brother is sick; he needs our help." The elders gathered at his home, and put up ceremonies on my behalf. Slowly I began to recover until one day I just walked out of the hospital.

In the meantime, my wife and I just drifted apart, and she found someone else. I became so angry that I went home and loaded my 22, and 22 magnum and my 30-30 rifles. I was going to go and shoot my wife and the man I thought she was running around with. As I was ready to walk out the door, I felt my mother's presence even though we were many miles apart. It made me stop in my tracks as I realized the consequences to the people I loved. I knew then that I had hit rock bottom. I suddenly realized just how broken I had become. That was when I decided to revisit my traditional teachings in earnest. My life's biggest journey was about to start.

Part 4
Healing Journey

Loon Lake Healing

My travels soon took me to Loon Lake. People from there had decided to go back to the traditional way of life. They wanted nothing to do with the whites. They refused everything, including alcohol. They would not take any money from anyone either. They would not participate in the white world in any way. They made their own knives and spears. They hunted and fished and dug up wild vegetables and picked berries. Paul Letendre continued to have sacred sweat lodges far out in the bush, even though he knew there was a risk of being jailed if caught. We had to stop the tea dances as it was not so easy to hide such a big event. The government did manage to stop us for years, as they threw people in jail for dancing, but today the dances have made a comeback. Tea Dances are more popular than ever. They could not wipe them out.

The traditional teachings continued. People gathered and listened to the wisdom keepers as they spoke of the traditional ways of thinking which had sustained us so well. Listening to the elders I started thinking about how these teachings could help me.

I began going through changes of feelings and emotions. I had felt empty, fearful, angry, and confused. I knew I could not continue my raging. I knew I had to make changes. Change is always difficult. I would be uplifted when a spark of understanding came to me. I spent more time quietly thinking and remembering.

I remembered the old teachings of the definition of a warrior and how it is much misunderstood. Some think it is related to being able to fight physically. It is much deeper than that. A true warrior lives in the light on the universal clock. The warrior is a role model and may be a teacher, a preacher, a doctor, or a councilor. The heroes were our peace officers who knew how to keep the peace without the use of force. The youth would look up to those persons and want to be like them when they grew up. My mother was a true warrior in every sense of the word. She was the hero, the mediator and a helper and student of ancient teachings. The warriors were the protectors, the guardians of all tribal members, as well as mediators for any situation that might arise. He or she was a master craftsman, the best hunter and marksman and a master survivalist under any conditions. All that, a warrior had to know to understand how to help in cases of conflict. All they did was for the good of all the tribal members. A warrior would be near the desired enlightenment level of being and sacrificed all for their beloved tribe. True warriors are at peace with themselves and confident in themselves. They do not have to threaten anyone to gain respect. Their actions would naturally bring respect. They are not controlled by others and have no self-doubt. They model those universal laws of morals, values, and ethics. What a true warrior does comes from within. If more people modelled that, there may not be so many violations of the man-made laws. As a warrior became older, they would teach others to follow in their footsteps so they too could move on in enlightenment.

This is a part of the circle of life, forever moving. I thought about becoming a warrior. That was much more suitable for me than raging. I just knew that I had a lot to learn before making any decisions for my future. At Loon Lake there were lots of warriors.

I began to see that I could not change others. It is their choice to be what they want to be, to think the way they choose. When I learned to be a free thinker, I also became much more aware of the choices I could make. I could choose to accept others as they are, or not. I could only make choices for myself and for my lifestyle.

When I realized that, others did not make me upset. I became aware that I chose to be upset when others did not understand or agree with me – it was a big step forward in my self-actualization. I did not have to like what another person does even if I didn't agree with them. I questioned if it was right to dislike others, or could I just ignore them and remove myself. I learned to make a distinction between what another person does versus what the other person believes. We are all human after all. Given the openness I was learning to live, I was discovering much about myself. I spent time looking inside and began to evaluate where my feelings of hurt and anger came from and what I could do to move on in a better way.

I began to follow the ancient teachings of first and foremost offering tobacco and gifting the elders with whatever I could. There was often a haunting sadness as I realized how much I had lost by raging. I also found profound joy as I began reconnecting with my Native identity. I listened and observed as the elders shared their truths. It was like I had lived and experienced the teachings in a remote past. Each wrinkled face, each gnarled hand, darkened by the sun and hard work, each movement had a story to tell. I just couldn't seem to get enough.

I realized I wanted to develop to the highest degree possible within the allotted time given for my physical life on earth. As I began to understand the serious nature of life, the will to grow in spirit became like an obsession. I began to contemplate how the threads of light that emanate both from within and without have a direct connection with nature beings and God Creator. Much of such mystical sharing was quite challenging because I would too often revert back to reason it out in our western-taught way of thinking.

The elders suggested that without some practical knowledge of self-worth, it may be quite difficult to bring those ideas or knowledge of worth into my heart and into everything I am. They told me that it was foolish to think that I, through my mental efforts alone, can make wholistic progress. The elders explained that through scientific explanation and western ways one squanders away his attention of his instinctual, heart and spiritual sides of his nature, wherein lies the real power of his being. In the attention to the ego some very important concepts and details which are important for self-development are often overlooked by the scientific mind. I had much to ponder about.

One afternoon I decided to go see my aunt Julian, who was a healer and living at Loon Lake at the time. Right away I knew that something was wrong. She tried to hide her tears, but she could not. When I asked her what had happened, she tearfully explained how she had come home and found all her medicines gone. Someone had taken them. A neighbour told her the Christian newcomers had come to her house and burnt them all. Her eyes were all red, so I knew she had been crying for a long time. I wanted to go and beat up every 'born again' for hurting my old auntie like that. She must have read my mind.

"Kiam," she said. "Let it go. Allow the Creator to take care of it." When she told me there would be karma for the terrible thing they had done, I could let it go. That was a huge step for me. I think that might have been the start of a much deeper understanding in my heart that violence was not the answer. I knew at that moment that I needed to work on myself and right then and there I began my true healing journey. I stayed some time with my Loon Lake friends. They would sing and dance, tell stories and laugh until the tears were rolling down their faces.

One of the favorite stories I remember was told over and over was about an old man who took a rope which was long enough to go around his waist five or six times. He took it with him every time he went hunting. It not only served to hold his pants up, but also came in handy for other things like leading or riding his horse. One day he went out hunting with his old muzzle loader gun. He was apparently after ducks or geese along a lake shore because he only brought the gun that would suffice for smaller game. To his surprise, he suddenly came across a black bear. He was not sure if it was going to attack or not. His gun was ready, but he had to determine if he had the fire power to kill the bear. As it wasn't too big, he decided he did. He proceeded to take great care in aiming and then squeezed the trigger. The bear dropped like he had been shot, which of course it had. The old man nudged and poked at that bear to make sure it was fatally wounded. There was plenty of blood on the ground and it did not move, so, the old man assured himself that today he would bring home a bounty. He unraveled his rope belt just enough so he could tie some around the bear's neck and the remainder of the rope, securely tied around his middle, served as his belt. He then proceeded to pull the bear home behind him. It was not such a big deal since he was about a half mile from help, and the bear was not yet full grown. At length the load seemed to get a lot lighter, to which the old man expressed delight and exclaimed "ah ha, I'm getting my second wind. I'm not so old after all." About that time, he turned around to view his prize, who was in turn looking back at him. His great aim and shot had apparently only grazed the bear, knocked him out and it had only now regained his senses. A great fear set in on the hunter and on his now alert prize. Each ran in opposite directions trying to get away from the other. The old man tried in vain to undo his belt and let the bear go. As the bouncing bear ran as fast as he could to get away, the old man could not untie his belt and he was dragged along to the nearest spruce tree. The bear shot up that tree thinking the old hunter was after him. The old man, needless to say, was pulled up the spruce tree by the rope on the bear, and the old man was getting a thrashing from the branches on his way up. Well about this time his rope belt decided to untie and so down he came, getting another thrashing from the branches.

It was said that he had only minor scratches and scrapes, but only from the branches, as he hobbled home, holding up his baggy pants since he no longer had his rope belt. However, when he got to the village, his story was that he had been in a hand-to-hand combat with a very large bear, but the bear ran for its life when he was starting to defeat him. No matter who told the story or how many times it would always bring a lot of laughter.

Our sense of humour kept us going. The more absurd the story, the more we laughed, and still do today. If I was to write these stories, they would make no sense because the body language would be missing. Some things are strictly for the spoken word and the sharing of feelings for one another. It is sort of like laughing alone. It just does not have the same effect as laughing together with someone. All good but different.

It was in Loon Lake that I became aware that life was worth living once again. Laughter was indeed the best medicine. When someone pulled a funny on someone else, we all knew how much that person cared. When someone teased another, it was one way of showing affection.

It was so good to be back with the elders. It brought back the feelings of caring and security of the days of my childhood. All the stories had a teaching. Each one is a precious memory. This story I am telling you now needs a quiet place to be told. Not in a restaurant. I need to find the right place. I see a park bench over there. That is ok.

A long time ago, there was a young lad who the community saw had great potential as a spiritual leader and a keeper of healing abilities. The community sent him to learn from an old wisdom keeper in the tribe. One day the young lad wandered off on his own. There was a stream which ran between two lakes. It was a fairly large stream with lots of fish. The young lad wanted to see more so he started jumping from rock to rock while the old man kept an eye on him. Suddenly the young lad stopped. "Mushum (Grandfather), come and see!! This it is fantastic!" he exclaimed pointing to the water, but the old man could see nothing out of the ordinary. He decided to join the young lad on the rock. When he got there, again he could see nothing out of the ordinary. Then the young lad said, "Mushum, just bend down and you will see it." The old man bent over and sure enough he saw the wonder the young lad was talking about. The moral of this story is: If you cannot see what someone else is seeing, go and stand on their rock and go to their level. Maybe you will feel what they are feeling. At that moment I knew I had to go and stand on other people's rocks.

One day I got restless again and left.

Peter O'Chiese

One morning I woke up from a restless sleep in my truck and headed for Robb, a small community in western Alberta, and thought I would stop there, but I started trembling and I knew something was wrong. I tried to turn the truck into a yard, but it would not turn. I decided maybe I better pray and ask for some direction. I did, then I knew where I was supposed to go. I drove on to the Kootenay Plains, no problem. The Kootenay Plains is a very sacred place for our people. They are located 67 km. west of Nordegg on Highway 11 in western Alberta. The beginning of the Rocky Mountains is directly west, and it is like the mountains are watching over and protecting these sacred grounds. We have attended ceremonies there for hundreds of years.

I drove up to a gate, which was closed, but something made me open it and I drove through to the other side. I got out of my truck and began walking aimlessly, remembering other times I had spent in this sacred place. I looked up and there I saw two teepees. As I stood there pondering who might be camping there, one of my teachers, Peter O'Chiese, suddenly appeared. "I think I am lost," I said. "You have just arrived," he said. "Come and join us." I only recognized one person that I knew, but everyone was laughing and sharing stories from the past. It just made my day.

Suddenly Peter motioned for me to follow him. I felt he wanted to say something important, so I did. I would not have done otherwise anyway, as he was a man of great wisdom. When we were out of earshot from the others, he told me in a caring voice, "time for you to go on a vision quest." I told him I was not prepared. I had come with nothing.

"You have come to find your spirit," said Peter quietly, pointing to a ridge on the mountain. "You will find it up there." Something in his voice made me not question his guidance. "First we will do a sweat lodge."

When we returned to the group, Peter's helpers immediately built the sweat lodge. They went looking for just the right willows and the perfect rocks. When they returned, some erected a frame and covered it with tarps and blankets, leaving an opening for a door. Others dug a hole in the middle. Still others built a fire to heat the rocks to red hot.

When the helpers were done we all entered the lodge on our hands and knees. The rocks were brought into the lodge and placed in the hole with prayer. The elder prayed with the prayer flags people brought. He was speaking Cree. The pipe was smoked. The doorway was covered. Water and medicine were poured on the rocks. We were in the darkness and dampness of the womb of Mother Earth. The elder chanted in Cree.

When I came out, everyone laughed at me. My wonderful warm sheepskin coat, which I had thought would keep me warm, was all burnt on one side. I giggled with them as well but was concerned because it gets very cold at night in the mountains, so I knew this was not good. I was also concerned about not having any sweetgrass, but I did have some northern incense, so I thought I would make that do.

I really was apprehensive as I did not have prayer prints, tobacco, or gifts for the elder, but he had told me I needed to go and find my spirit on the mountain, so I had to go – I could not disobey his instructions. I was given an old tarp and told to find the place where I was going to sit out. I was given a braid of sweetgrass to take along, so I could smudge with it. To make sure it was not lit any more, I rubbed it on my cheek. It was definitely out. I put it in my pocket. Just as I was finished preparing my sacred place I looked down and there was a big hole burnt in my other jacket. I guess the spirits really wanted me to suffer, I thought.

After sitting for over a week without food or water, I learned something as I entered a different reality. Peter did come and talk to me off and on. He reminded me about the traditional ways of non-interference, of love-based teachings of life. I guess he knew what I needed. Once again, I was reminded about what was important in life was given to us by the Creator and Mother Earth. The rest was only good for temporary satisfaction. I spent a lot of time with Peter over the years. I learned from him how to tell the difference between those elders who were genuine and those who were just faking. That is those who had not done the work and did not have the depth of teachings needed to be a genuine elder. He would say that faking it by behaviour sucks. I called these 'popcorn elders.'

Peter used to teach anyone of any race as long as they were in a good place of wanting to learn in earnest. It was from Peter that I learned that all people regardless of race or where they came from or where they were going deserved the opportunity to learn the Creator's teachings. It would be a much better world if others understood the peaceful way of non-interference, of respect for all people. Of those who were not true to themselves, who pretended to want to learn, he would say, "Don't bother with those people. They will just waste your time and they are not worth it."

When Peter got older, I used to go and take care of him, because he took care of me when I needed it.

Chief Smallboy

I first visited Chief Smallboy when he was camped out at the Kootenay plains. In 1959 Chief Smallboy took some 150 followers and moved to the Kootenay Plains to get away from the reality of the restrictions imposed on his people. Their hunting grounds had been allocated to white settlers and were no more. Education was provided by the newcomers and did not in any way reflect the ancient ways of education which had sustained us for so many generations. Smallboy was quite aware of the benefits of the western education, however and wanted to set up an education system based on the traditional teachings and the western system combined. He also wanted to take his followers away from the new reality of drugs, alcohol, and political turmoil as experienced on the reservation. He wanted to return to the traditional way of life. A way of life based on the spiritual teachings of the ancestors, but also recognizing and incorporating the reality of the changes. He and his followers were in pursuit of freedom. There had been a prediction many years prior that when the blood of Mother Earth would be sold, it would bring spiritual and physical sickness. He wanted to protect his people the best he could.

The flock had just moved in four months prior to my first visit, so they were still in the process of adjusting to the old way of life. Trapper's tents were erected for every family. Each had a little cook stove in it made from metal. These stoves were very light weight and shaped like a square, with four holes on top covered by lids which could be taken off to add more wood or left off and the hole covered by a cooking pot for more heat. Members had brought them along from Hobbema. Chief Smallboy also set up a big tent which was used as a school. There the children learned the ways of the ancestors as well as how to read and write English. Later he moved his flock further back into the wilderness east of the Rockies, where his descendants and those of his followers remain today.

Chief Smallboy predicted the downfall of his people if they followed the 'white' ways. If they took the easy way of the instant gratification of liquor and drugs. He believed the oil money would be the root of evil. It has proven out to be the truth. He talked about how if a young buck had his eye on a young maiden, he would go to her grandmother and sing his declaration for his intent to her. He would ask her to speak for him with her family. The family would in turn talk to the young maiden to see how she felt about the union. Her grandparents would speak to the young buck's family and if everyone agreed that they would be good together, each would begin a time of apprenticeship. Only when the grandparents felt the couple was ready, could they move together. There was a strong code which only allowed one mate for life, so the grandparents wanted to see their grandchildren live in harmony for the upcoming faces, for their community and for themselves. The grandmothers and grandfathers would need to see that their grandchildren would be brought up in a good way. Hearing his words, I began recalling the teachings of my mother, my aunties, and grandparents back in the days of my life at Lubicon Lake.

One day, many years later, I decided that it was time to pay a visit to the Smallboy camp again. Chief Smallboy was getting old by that time. He had met with world leaders including our queen, our prime minister, Pierre Elliot Trudeau, and others. He was so instrumental in trying to help others understand, in trying to build bridges for all. He did not have much success in Ottawa, the seat of the Canadian government, however much he tried. Before his passing he was given an audience with the Pope. When he began to explain about the land grab, the corruption of the newcomers, the problems faced by our people he listened intently, but when he brought up the abuse in the residential schools, a cardinal quickly came and whisked the Pope away.

After his passing in 1984, I decided to pay his camp a visit one more time. That was a most difficult visit. After his death outsiders came to his camp. Things began to change. The members had abandoned the appointment of the 'headmen' traditional way of choosing leaders. The introduction of the vote brought chaos within the political system as was evident in many other native communities. Drugs and alcohol had once again raised their ugly heads. I think the majority had abandoned their traditional ways, but not all. It was hard to see. Smallboy's vision was broken. I left with a heavy heart.

Elders

The next few years I spent much time sitting with the elders and taking in their teachings.

Mother Earth is for all people, no one could own Her. She is our Mother. I remember the old people saying that we were Her children and we belonged to Mother Earth. Our people understood the interdependency with a healthy environment for our food, our water and for life itself. We were all conscientious of our connection to the divine and the earthly family.

The teepee was also a large part of that balance. Eddie Bellerose and I sat one day and put to paper the meaning of each teepee pole and why erecting a teepee was also like a sacred ceremony. We would pray that all the people who entered would be blessed with the meaning of each of these poles.

The elders know the power of Mother Earth, plants, and animals. They know the power of the Great Spirit. They understand how to use this power to help and heal all, and I needed more healing. I knew I had to be stronger in order to accomplish my new mission. I made offerings to the elders in order to access the help I needed and the knowledge and strength I craved from Creator, the star people and all the good entities who could help. We learn from those who went before us, and we pass our knowledge on to those who follow us. That is the way it is. Now was my time to learn from the old ones.

The old have much time to meditate and learn things. The autumn years are a time of wisdom. The old ones have walked this earth for so many years and experienced much. Still, they say they only know so little. The teachings were passed down verbally from generation to generation for thousands of years.

THE TEEPEE

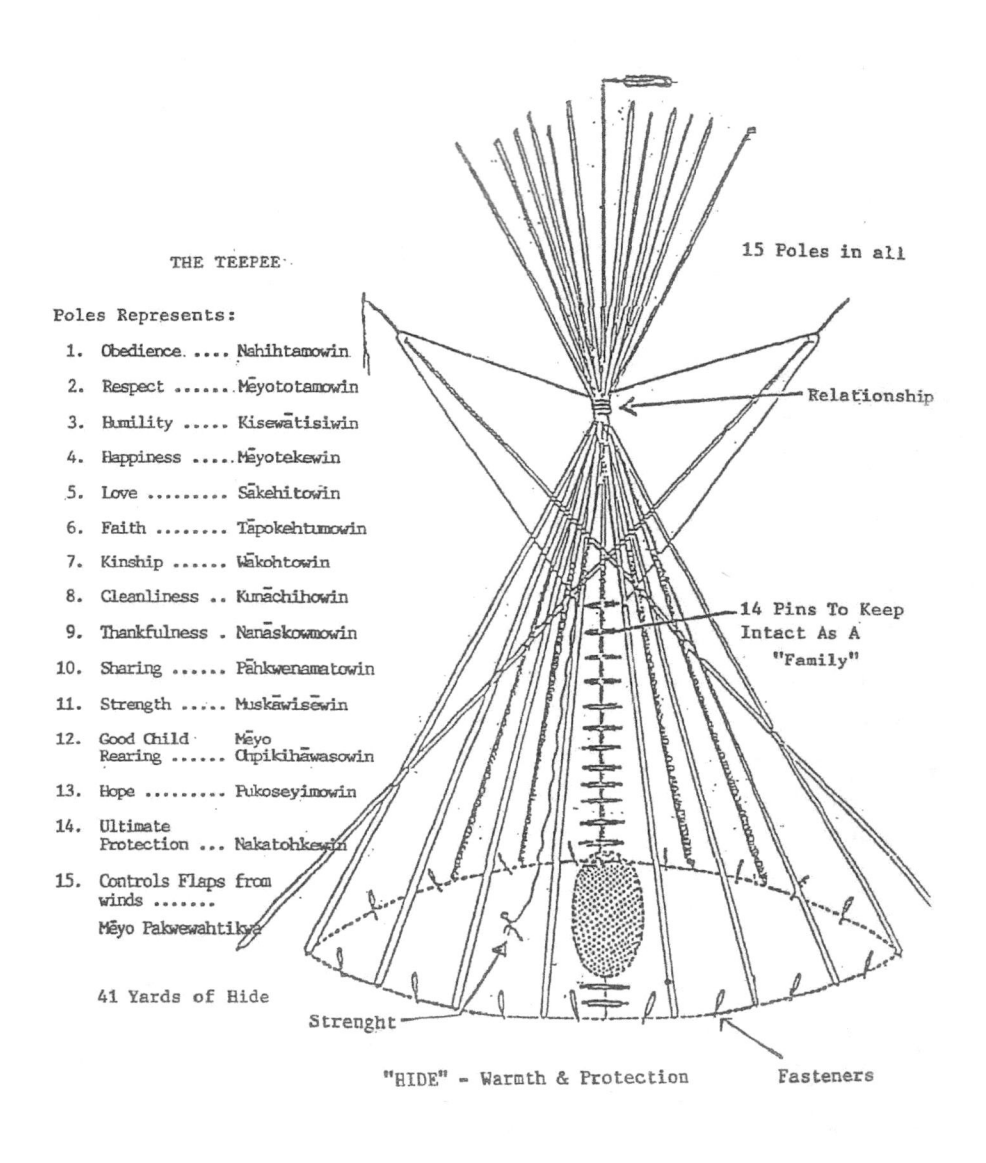

Poles Represents:

1. Obedience ..... Nahihtamowin
2. Respect .... Meyototamowin
3. Humility ..... Kisewatisiwin
4. Happiness .... Meyotekewin
5. Love .... Sakehitowin
6. Faith .... Tapokehtumowin
7. Kinship ...... Wakohtowin
8. Cleanliness .. Kunachihowin
9. Thankfulness . Nanaskowmowin
10. Sharing ...... Pahkwenamatowin
11. Strength ..... Muskawisewin
12. Good Child Meyo
    Rearing ..... Ohpikihawasowin
13. Hope .... Pukoseyimowin
14. Ultimate
    Protection ... Nakatohkewin
15. Controls Flaps from
    winds ....
    Meyo Pakwewahtikwa

41 Yards of Hide

15 Poles in all

Relationship

14 Pins To Keep
Intact As A
"Family"

Strenght

"HIDE" - Warmth & Protection

Fasteners

Meaning of the teepee poles

The elders I sat with have much to share with those who wish to learn. Each day brings about new wisdom, as well as opportunity to grow. For the wisdom keepers there is no end point, no graduation if you will, no certificates. The seeking to evolve, to expand their knowledge base is never ending. I had so much reverence for these elders who are the fact keepers, the historians, and the law keepers. Laws are derived from the Great Spirit which manifest in the laws of nature and the universe.

The elders taught everyone to live by the seven gifts or laws as they were passed by the 'Grandfathers' (from the spirit world) many generations ago. They would teach how to live with respect, love, courage, honesty, humility, wisdom, and truth. If anyone strayed from these gifts, they would get a teaching that they were not likely to forget.

The elders told me that if any of the seven gifts cause too much pressure on your feelings and emotions, something needs to be taken care of. Something needs to be learned. These gifts helped guide me to be the best I can be. I am far from perfect, but I try.

The old ones explained how important it was to remember that one's own morals and values are ethics, and those ethics determine the state of our spirit, or consciousness. Ethics are you, in you. Your instincts and intuition are connected to your ethics in that they determine how much understanding you can gain when your spirit is healthy. If the spirit is not healthy, one will not be able to grasp the spiritual knowledge that is meant for you.

Another lesson I learned from the elders was to keep your power centers clear in order to enhance intuition and instincts. They explained that when you are clear and open you can discern positive from negative in people. Your emotions, your spiritual self is all used to 'read' another person. If all is well with yourself, you will never be mistaken. This will happen with proper behaviour and attitude and by maintaining inner peace and harmony.

A story from the ancients would prove the power of truth by smudging a sharp bone knife, and then holding it to the sun. Then they would pass the sharp edge of the knife slowly over their tongue. If it was not cut it was proof of the truth. When the Europeans first came, and they tried to prove they were telling the truth with the knife. They cut themselves. My people knew they were twisting the truth. That is where the saying "paleface speak with forked tongue" originated. When the legal system was thrust upon us, it began using the swearing on the bible. Because there are no physical signs of untruths, for us that method could not be trusted. We are taught that the spoken word is sent out to the Universe like radio waves. The Elders always reminded us to speak truthfully and softly and never condemn nor swear at others. The nasty words you send out there will come back to haunt you.

A person who is angry, has low self-esteem, low levels of acceptance and tolerance might think they are able to use intuition, but they are not. Before a person is ready to receive Creator's teachings, they must be pure in body, mind, and spirit. If they abuse their God given sexual powers, if they do not think with clarity and allow bad thoughts to enter their mind, there will not be room for the good and productive messages to come through. If the spirit is not healthy or abusive a person will not receive the messages that can be theirs. That is the purpose of sacrifice. It is to open one-self to receive.

Soon after I returned to the life I was meant to live, I was in a room with many people arguing fiercely about political issues; I observed a couple of elders being cool, calm, and collected. When I asked one elder how he could stay so calm, he said, "My grandson, when one knows Creator, they cannot help but be at peace." I thought that I could never reach that calmness. The elders sit quietly and wait for the return to the truth of the ancestral teachings if they so wish to learn more. They sit and wait for the seekers to come.

Some seekers are lost for their whole lives, some return. Maybe the lost will learn more in the after-life time. If my mind was open to receiving on every level, I felt great, and my spirit would soar with the new knowledge. When I feel good, I can think good – when I think good, I feel good. I guess you can call it a kind of medicine wheel, or a catch 22 for the good things. As I became aware of these gifts and gave them my full attention, I began to lead a positive life. In that state of mind, I could learn much.

I learned that it was always important to pay attention and evaluate my feelings when something was not right. I learned from the negative as well as the positive. There is always a lesson in everything.

One thing I was taught by the elders was that if someone is angry and giving you a tongue lashing, there is an imbalance between you. My first job was to listen intently to what is being said. Then look at myself to really see if I have done anything wrong. If I have, then I had to try to make amends with that person so we both can get back to a good place again. If I concluded that I did not deserve the tongue lashing, then maybe the other person has a problem and that person may need some help to reach balance. Meeting anger with anger just escalates a situation. Getting angry myself accomplishes nothing. In my anger I would lose my power, and neither would be good for the other. It is hard to remain calm, but I slowly learned that if I got hurt or angry, I may not have the strength to fix the situation in a good way. In that case I would have to walk away.

The elders warned about tampering with earth, water, wind/air, or fire because these are our creation's life support systems. Life as we know it is interdependent, each on the other. We need each other and the four elements to survive.

The modern devices such as cell phones, video games and too much TV interfere with the ability to stay in balance. I remember the elders teasing the kids that too much radio and later TV was all mechanical and would give them bald heads. The moral value systems have deteriorated badly as technology has progressed in leaps and bounds. Where should we place the most attention? On materialistic items that we cannot take along in death or those other important matters that will follow us even after death? One who knows will limit these devices.

Once you have this knowledge embedded in your soul in all your being, you are a free spirit, no longer dependent on anything or anyone for your fulfillment. Then you've got it. I became closely connected to God, Creator. Love became the life force and the path I did my best to walk from one day to the next. No one is perfect, but I tried. At least I began understanding what it meant to walk the good red road.

The elders, before being restricted, had travelled freely throughout the continent, and exchanged medicines and stories. Now they could not. New diseases were appearing that no one had medicines for. I think that was one of the most difficult adjustments the old people had to make after contact.

The old ones reminded us all, that what we seek is within the seeker. I was reminded that the Great Mystery, Creator, or Great Spirit is everywhere and in all creation. That is what was revealed to the ancient Native prophets and so be it. The Great Mystery's spark of selfhood lies within every man, woman, and child. A Native person of worth does not speak of that which he or she does not know to be true, and the ancients have said that this is to be so. If one becomes egotistical, they are going against the teachings of the ancients and there will be consequences for their discretion. They will not know peace. When I was raging, I knew no peace.

To a traditional person, their word is their bond. Words once spoken are to be taken as sacred. I would never hear a traditional person curse or swear. Only those who have lost their way and been westernized would be reckless with their words. There are no swear words in my traditional Cree language. It is our ancient belief that as a man thinks, so he is. As a man feels, so he is. As a man moves, so he is. As a man hears, so he is. As a man is spirited, so he is. As a man is, so goes his relationship with his God, Creator, mankind, and all Creation. With that purpose is the whole domain of his life.

The lodge teachings were that it is not enough to know, it is not enough to say the words, it is not enough to pray verbally, it is not enough to be 'outwardly' kind and loving. One must do what he or she knows to be good, with their whole mind, body, heart, and spirit. It must all relate to inner peace and harmony and move outward. One must understand the unseen power of the Creator. Then the light given is the life given.

When you know the sacred teachings, you are in balance and there is no need for talk about forgiveness. It is life for those who know. Many of my people do not know this. This is much deeper than alcohol and drugs, which have no place in the celebration of life as passed to us by the star people.

There is much more that could be said about the Elders, but I will leave it at that for now. Another Native person who has seen and experienced their roots, traditions, principles, and practices of the ancients will come forward with more insights.

After sitting with the elders and listening to them I was able to turn my life around. I became aware my younger years would not have been so challenging had I not turned away from their teaching in the first place. Going back to the elder's teachings got my life back in balance. Learning to pay attention to the seven gifts of emotional balance made my life worth living and gave me the strength to help others. Every day I thank the Creator for my enlightenment, for Creator's teachings and support. From the elders I learned what being a true Native person really is.

Being a true Native person is not about owning a treaty number, it is not just a matter of blood lines, it is not just a matter of language, it is not just a matter of moose hides and buffalo robes. It is so much deeper than that. It is much more than our dances and ceremonies. I learned that the understanding of the importance of 'spirit in the body', not a 'body with a spirit' is utmost. Once a person understands that and allows the spirit to guide daily activities, life becomes good. If I allowed myself to be guided by the Great Spirit, honour and be honoured, I could walk a good path.

Basic Personality Types

The elders taught me about the four basic personality types. First level we encounter is the angry, very aggressive, out of harmony being. I was taught that this is the lowest level of man. He is not one bit enlightened. He understands nothing when it comes to spiritual enlightenment. He is argumentative and will always insist he is right. They are most likely bullies. They will use vulgarity in order to express themselves because their way is the right way no matter what opinion anyone else has. Some people are very uncomfortable in their presence and will remove themselves from that energy. The person who is out of balance will display tunnel vision and will not listen to other's points of view. These people are often hated by others who are not enlightened. They struggle to function well on the job or in their homes. They are schemers and are often wealthy as they do not have the personality to care about anyone. I have also found that these people are generally very racist.

The enlightened person needs to be cautious and not retaliate, or they will draw themselves down to the first level of humanness. Sometimes the people in their presence suffer from very low self-esteem. It is so difficult to love such a person and only the most enlightened can do that. The true elders will pray for these people to learn to change their ways. Because these lowest levels of people lack empathy, they are not capable of love. The attraction to others is basically physical and intellectual, with absence of emotional and spiritual. This lowest level of being has not yet reached the ability to know oneself.

The second level of being is withdrawn and very shy. This person would generally not be able to set goals and those who do would rarely reach them anyway. The second level of people are often the targets of bullies as the bullies always look for an easy target. If such a person is pushed too far, they will suddenly rise up and defend themselves. I have seen the elders and the parents and siblings, and friends try to implant into that person some self-esteem. In a spiritual way the second level people are not far from the first level, but the major difference is that the second level people would not show much aggression. Although it is hard to convince them to change behavior, it is not impossible, given enough support. They too are not capable of love, as they have no love for themselves. They too will be attracted to another person only on a physical or intellectual level with a bit of emotion, but the spiritual aspect seems to be completely absent. This level has not yet been in touch with self-discovery.

The third level of being is generally outgoing, but not aggressive or bullying. They may be seen to be pretty well balanced. They are most likely friendly and gentle overall. They are closer to enlightenment than the first and second level. Third level people will never intentionally hurt others. They are open to have others in their lives and they will seek out help because of their good attitude and behaviour. They are generally good problem solvers and have some life skills. Third level people have empathy for others so are aware of the effect their behaviour has on others. They are able to make decisions which are harmonious to themselves and others. This third level of people can be attracted to others emotionally, intellectually, and physically and may even have some spiritual connection. They can experience both conditional and unconditional love from others in the same level. This level of being has moved into self-discovery and self-knowledge. They do have self-mastery over their own ethics and are aware of negative consequences. They are close to moving on to enlightenment.

The highest developed person would be a kind and caring person. This can be observed as they radiate that through their physical, and especially through their eyes. Each person who meets someone in this highest level will feel that kindness when they are in their presence. This level will have unconditional love for other humans and all life. There was a time when many of my people reached this level, but today with all the distractions too many do not put in the time and sacrifices it takes to reach such a level. This is the desired level of all spiritual leaders and teachers of life, but few achieve total kindness and love for all. It would mean letting go of many attitudes from the past, including the attachment to possessions and intellectual ideas which may not be suitable in this highest state. They would never have any feelings of superiority over God's/Creator's creations. They would send a power of love and joy to others, and they would have it returned. This highest level, the enlightened person, knows and understand the laws of attraction. This was the level I dreamed of reaching.

The Eagle Teachings

The eagle is a wonderful teacher of balance. The head represents the elders. The eyes of the future, the leaders, the visionaries. They have the clearest perspective. Wings are the parents, riding the winds calm or turbulent. Tail feathers represent the youth, flying in the same direction as the parents and the elders. The body represents the children. The heart and soul protected and sheltered on all sides. So, they can flourish, grow, and explore. When any part of the eagle is broken or hurt, it cannot fly. An important teaching incorporated to create the balance necessary to move on in a good way. Another most powerful teaching was about balance as taught to us by the eagle feather. Looking straight on, one will see that the feather is divided into two segments, one on each side of the solid center. There are many teachings, but these are the ones I was taught.

When we look at the eagle feather held upside down the teachings are that one side is a reminder of what the ancients shared with us, and the other side stood for good human morals, values, and ethics, in our relationship to all others. It was a reminder that we must behave properly and have good attitudes toward our fellow man. It was a reminder of our responsibility to be good workers and providers for our loved ones and our communities. With the invasion came the necessity to learn new skills, but the teachings of the eagle feather remain just as valid as ever.

Now if we turn the feather right side up, the broad side was a reminder that we must always remember our God or Creator and live our lives according to Creator's teachings. As we turn our attention to the narrow side, we are reminded that there is also evil in this world. Created either by man or by the negative from the spirit world. One was reminded to pay attention to who or what was creating a situation, the good or the bad. We had a choice, but the ancients always encouraged us to follow the Creator's ways of the good.. The consequences of either way would be revealed in our actions.

The elders shared how the eagle feather teachings are based on sacred place, sacred space. They are teachings about connectedness and harmony with all.

One does not go out and kill an eagle in order to get a feather. If one has earned the right, he may get one from an elder or an eagle may actually drop a feather for a person who has earned it. I so wanted my own eagle feather, but the elders I sat with did not pass me one and eventually it became quite an annoyance for me. I knew I shouldn't feel that way, but I couldn't help it. One day I was standing under a tree, deep in thought when suddenly an eagle feather came floating down in front of me. I looked up in time to see that eagle disappear into the sky. I had to leave tobacco as an offering of my gratefulness. I also said a prayer of gratitude to the eagle for the gift that it made.

If a tribe member had accomplished a worthy task, he or she could be honored with a presentation of an eagle feather. A man may get to carry one or more eagle feathers if he accomplished something extra ordinary like saving a person's life or being able to help with medicines which may be spiritually passed to him or being an extra-ordinary good hunter and bringing meat to those who could not hunt for themselves.

Unfortunately, some of our non-traditional people have forgotten or were not taught this basic principle. Some radical and militant people are not humble and do not know the true teachings of the eagle feather. They will often walk around showing off their feathers. That is not the purpose. There are however two other significant exceptions A smaller eagle feather, or a plume, may be given to a person to signify that they are a helper to an elder, or a student who has committed to learning the way of the sacred walk. You will most often see them being worn at ceremonies but can also be worn at other times. It is a recognition that he is a student, and it is by wearing the feather that he is recognized as such. Those who traveled in search of their teachers and carried the small feather or plume would be given full cooperation to connect to the right teachers. The plumes could be carried when maneuvering their way through this modern world. It helped give the wearer strength and reminded the wearer to bring the ancient teachings with them wherever they went.

Those who misuse their sexual gifts or do not earn the right to a mate and bring children into this world or have many partners or produce children that they do not look after properly should not be feather holders.

A person cannot fool an elder into thinking he had earned his feather. A true elder cannot be fooled. They will see through the deception and may give that person a very uncomfortable teaching. No one can hide from the Creator or a true elder, and that person may suffer lots in his teachings about deceit. The deceptive person will eventually be exposed, or the feather will leave them. I know of instances where eagle feathers have disappeared from the person carrying them if they do not live up to the code of life.

Traditional Education

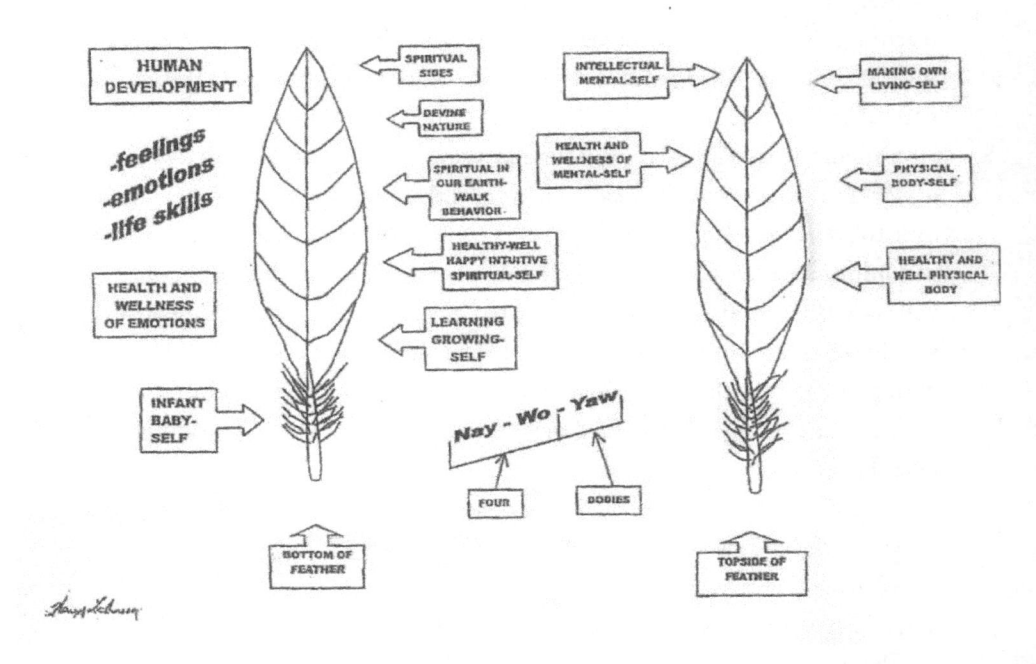

- HUMAN DEVELOPMENT
- feelings
- emotions
- life skills
- HEALTH AND WELLNESS OF EMOTIONS
- INFANT BABY-SELF
- BOTTOM OF FEATHER

- SPIRITUAL SIDES
- DEVINE NATURE
- SPIRITUAL IN OUR EARTH-WALK BEHAVIOR
- HEALTHY-WELL HAPPY INTUITIVE SPIRITUAL-SELF
- LEARNING GROWING-SELF

- INTELLECTUAL MENTAL-SELF
- HEALTH AND WELLNESS OF MENTAL-SELF

- MAKING OWN LIVING-SELF
- PHYSICAL BODY-SELF
- HEALTHY AND WELL PHYSICAL BODY
- TOPSIDE OF FEATHER

Nay - Wo - Yaw
FOUR BODIES

These teachings and others do vary slightly from tribe to tribe, but the foundation of the deep truth is the same. These things I share with you are the way I was taught. Others may have different teachings. After I learned these things, life got much better as I could begin to stand in my power.

Nature Teachings

Our people always learned from nature and all our relations including Mother Earth, the animals large and small, all the flying, swimming, and the crawling. The plants also taught us many things.

The elders spoke much about how we could learn from the creatures in nature. We could also learn from the four seasons and the four directions. These teachings I got with sitting in sacred circles, from the sacred medicine wheel, or the sacred hoop. These teachings would encompass the universal laws and the natural order of life.

Our ancestors learned to read the signs and in turn taught us. That's the way it works. The leaves of the black poplar and the willow trees will turn slightly over to signal to all creatures that rain is coming. That gives them time to take the appropriate action to protect themselves. The small birds like the sparrow will have their food safely stored close to the ground before a rain. When the weather is going to be nice and warm, they would be swooping and playing with each other in the skies. The movements and the songs of the birds change with the upcoming storms. That way all humans and animals would know to take shelter.

Larger birds fly in circles high in the sky in a clockwise or counterclockwise direction depending on the upcoming weather. There is much more, but I am just sharing a little to give you the idea that my people knew lots from nature and adjusted our lives according to the signs shared by birds and trees.

The wisdom keepers observed which birds coupled together and who took care of the young. How one day they became mates for each other. One mate for life was learned from such observations. The wisdom keepers knew that in most species, if one died, the other would remain alone for the rest of their lives.

One exception is the Canada goose. They will seek out a widow or widower to be together with, but only if they were not related would they accept each other to have a family. Us humans were taught not to cheat on husbands or wives as the big birds did not do that. Somehow, they knew not to have offspring with close relations. Each creature knew what to do to survive and not overpopulate.

All this I learned when I sat with the elders. My people observed all and learned from all. As the wise ones observed the bear, they saw which plants and roots were edible. My ancestors called the bear the 'four-legged person' – so what was good for the bear is good for the people. They also called the bear the 'doctoring animal' because they learned the healing herbs from the bear. Some bear parts were also good medicine, but no one would ever take down a bear without its permission. This was done through ceremonies.

Bears in the wilderness gave birth to their cubs in the dens in the middle of winter. They understood when they needed to procreate for the survival of their young. They would leave the den in the spring and the mother bear would teach the young how to survive on their own. After one more winter in the den the young would leave their mother. Just as with humans, it is the parents' job to teach the young ones to function on their own. It is not right to keep them dependent. The young must leave to find their own mate and have young to carry on from one generation to the next.

Circle

The circle is evident in all aspects of our lives, as the ancestors used the sacred talking circle, the healing circle, the sweat lodges and sun dance lodges. All built circular. Even the birds build their nests in the round. Then and now. In the circle of life there has always been this one consistency.

Nothing in nature is linear. Days are a cycle from daylight through darkness and back to daylight. The earth rotates around the sun. Not linear to the sun. Each moon is a cycle from new moon to full moon and back to darkness only to begin the cycle again. That was the calendar we were taught to follow. It worked well.

Even life was a circular journey with the babies being close to the Creator. As people move up the circle, they continually learn from those who went before. Then as people moved around through middle age, the younger adults naturally took over the duties of those who passed before. Everyone's duty was to pass on advice and guidance to those who came after. That is the cycle of life. Everyone was a student of the ones that had went before and a teacher to the ones who came after. As we move into the time of the completion of our life, having come full circle, we were once more closer to the Creator. Both the new and the old were teachers of the spirit world.

The wisdom keepers observed the positions of the stars and their cycles of when and where they appeared. They understood the rotation of the earth from season to season. Through their observations they understood the natural order of things. The wisdom keepers saw the manifestation of order brought by the Great Spirit. I just could not get enough of these teachings. There was so much to learn. I was hungry for the knowledge.

Seven Power Centers

Another teaching that was so important to our personal wellbeing was about the seven power centers. The chakras, as they are called today, are very important to your balance and wellbeing. The first power center is at the top of your head. It is very tender, and we are to take care what we put into our minds as that affects the other six power centers. If this is open, it will be a channel to open communication between yourself and the star people.

The second power center is located in the center of the forehead just above the eyebrow line. This power center is very much dominant with the spiritual, instinct and intuition. The elders taught us that those people who have visions that others can't see comes through this power center. Some people today will call it the third eye. All people have this second power center, but many just shrug it off as imagination and will therefore not pursue the understanding further. Meditation and proper learning will enable a person to see into the past, present and future. One elder remarked. "There is so much to see and so few who care to look."

The third power center is located at the vocal cord area. The spoken word is very powerful, both positive and negative. The old ones say that your word is your bond and affects all power centers, so therefore words must always be true.

The fourth power center is the heart. The old ones insist that each heartbeat must beat the rhythm of the four major directions. One must relate fully, respect fully, be honest with all and everything. We must be humble at all times. It means that the person fully in this power is in the unconditional love life force. The most powerful force of all. Love is a life force on its own. The elders shared that disease, unhappiness, and despair is a result of a violation of the of the law of love. One's tone of voice will reflect attitude and it will reveal one's own spiritual level of being. If one violates any of the teachings, they will regress to a lower level. If that happens, one is in great need of help, or they will hurt others and especially themselves. If the heart center is off balance, the other six power centers will also be affected and injured in the process. A pure heart is a state of wellbeing and balance. There is no other way to happiness.

The fifth power center is the seat of emotion and is situated just above the navel. The old ones say that feelings are picked up at this location. When we hear, see, touch, taste or smell something, the feelings picked up are moved at that power center. Intuition and instinct are close to the fifth power center. They are often overlooked by those who do not know this. The notion that things are good or not good will be felt at this power center. If in the presence of something not good, a person at the highest level of consciousness will have to physically remove himself or herself from the situation or they will get hurt.

The sixth power center is the seat of the spirit and is located just below the belly button. The old ones say that when the spirit is moved it impacts the emotion, and we will feel the full impact both spiritually and emotionally at all the power centers. That in turn also affects our body and our mind. When the spirit moves us, everything is put into motion. This is connected to 'butterflies in the stomach.' It will test our confidence in ourselves to the fullest. Most emotion, although felt in the area of the fifth power center, is driven by the sixth. Intuition and instinct are very much connected to this power center. When we can connect that with thought and feeling, we may be well tuned in and will understand messages passed from Creator and nature beings. From this knowledge, we will understand that everything was created perfect. The Universe is perfect, and we are a part of that perfection. The Universe and nature and our inner self are all in harmony in that state. Those who know this understand that the connection with all is a connection with the true source of being. Are we then a spirit with a body or a body with a spirit? The elders truly understood the importance of our spirit as connecting with Creator and the universe, and our bodies are condensed matter connected to Mother Earth. We are a part of the greater universe and everything that is.

The seventh power center is the seat of humanity and of life creation. It is located in the genital area. The old ones do not speak much of this power center because of the location. It is one of those topics that may be too sacred to share with a young person of the opposite sex. This discussion would only be with the same sex person. For instance, the grandmothers with this knowledge would talk to the young women or girls and the grandfathers would talk to the young men or boys. Nothing would ever be said in mixed company. Everyone honored the women as the givers of new life, but the men would also be honoured as they provide the seed for the new life. Men and women are co-creators with the Creator. You did not have sexual relations until your teachings were complete and the elders felt that you were ready for this sacred responsibility. Understanding how this power center was connected to life itself was a part of that teaching.

Each must be healthy and flowing with goodness in order to be the best one can be. One had to be prepared to be a good provider and a good home maker as well as being knowledgeable about the spiritual laws and the power centers which could then in turn be passed on to the next generation and in turn safeguard the strength of the communities and all humanity. The effects of the priests and nuns violating this sacred space has haunted countless numbers of my people, some for their whole lifetime.

The knowing that we are co-creators and certain knowledge must be understood and followed and keeping the seven power centers healthy is of utmost importance to all humanity. To do less is unpardonable according to nature laws. There was much to absorb, and I so wanted to do my very best.

Following is a tale often told many times in wherever I went. We just never got enough of listening to these stories. Many lessons were taught through story telling. This story is a teaching about power of gentleness and the help of the star people.

Indian Maiden's Legend

There was one small village that had found their center and lived accordingly. This meant that the collective village and all its members lived in total harmony and cooperation with themselves, their village members and Creator and Mother Earth. The Creator had passed the guidance and they listened. This village was not large or over-populated. It was regarded as being just right. All parents had earned the right to be mates. They had earned to right to be parents to all the children born in the village. Everyone followed the natural law of having no more than four children, one for each direction. These were the times of quality upbringing as opposed to quantity. Every man and woman knew their place. Every boy or girl were taught how not to overstep their place as well. In this small village there lived a young man and a young woman. They regarded each other with high esteem. It was understood that one day they would wed.

Nearby there lived many other tribes. These other large tribes had fallen off the path given to them by ancients. They had decided to follow their own man-made laws. They fought with each other and with other tribes. The men took mates whether they deserved them or not. They overpopulated. There was much in quantity, but questionable quality of child rearing and upbringing. Their moral and value systems as well as ethics was lacking as was demonstrated by behaviour and attitude. They had forgotten what a true Native person is supposed to be.

The people in the larger village were mean and warlike and posed a problem for the small and peaceful tribe. They regressed lower and lower toward the lowest form of being. The once sacred ceremonies became distorted and lost more meaning. They were moving toward demon worship and barbarianism, away from the light and toward darkness. The time did come when the large mean tribe harassed the small tribe. The small tribe took it all in hand and held their ground the day the large warlike tribe attacked the small tribe. The fighting was fierce, but the large mean tribe pulled back as their loss was great. When that day of fighting was over the small peaceful tribe suffered only minor scratches and bruises, and so ended that day.

In the small peaceful tribe, the young maiden and the young warrior began preparing for their future together. There were many well-wishers and blessings bestowed on them by tribal elders. There was much preparation in store for the pairing of the young woman and man. But the thought of the warlike tribe was not far away. The small peaceful tribe remained on guard.

One day the young warrior took the young maiden aside and spoke deeply with her. The young warrior told her that the warlike tribe was bothering his thoughts. He said to her that if he should not survive the next attack, he would leave her something to make good thoughts and memories for her and the tribe.

It came to pass that the small peaceful tribe was once again attacked by the warlike tribe. This confrontation was fiercer than any other before. The small tribe fought back with great valor and emotion. They had something worth defending and fighting for and dying for. The tribes fought all that morning and into the late afternoon. It was seen when the fighting was over that for every one of the small peaceful tribe warriors killed, four or five of the of the larger warlike tribe members were killed. As the sun was making its descent that fateful day, the warriors of the small tribe that did not return to the circle of the camp were in the thoughts and hearts of everyone. The tribal elders sent the relatives of the warriors to the place of battle to pick up their warriors' remains. The young maiden committed to the young warrior was among those who went to the battle place.

The young maiden searched and searched and finally did find her beloved young warrior. He had lived and died as he had believed. He gave his life to prevent the poison of ignorant and arrogant warlike ways to enter into the peaceful yet strong tribe. It is said that there were nearly a dozen of the warlike tribe members lying around him where he was found. The young maiden took her unmoving warrior to her lap and cried. With deep long breaths she wept many tears remembering what she and her warrior might have been. In time she wiped her eyes and wept no more. The memories of what the young warrior had said entered her mind and she looked around to see what it was that he had left behind for her. She could not find anything, and she raised her face and eyes to the skies and cried out, "What is it, what has my beloved left behind?" As she did so, her hands touched the earth, and she felt her fingertips going among small pebble-like yet smoother objects. As she looked to the ground where her tears had fallen, she saw dark pearl-like yet clear objects. Today these pebbles are known as the Indian teardrops or Apache teardrops, and they bring good thoughts and memories. They represent the small yet strong peaceful tribe that had followed all good teachings to live in harmony and cooperation as guided by our Creator of all. This story, in due time, echoed throughout the land. No more was that peaceful tribe bothered by any other hostilities. May the tears and trials of our forefathers not be in vain.

Part 5
Wanderings

Old Teepees

One day I was driving through the bush east of our village looking for game. There were old trails all through that area from when the white people were looking for natural resources. I have to say I did appreciate those old roads. I had an old Ford truck which would go almost anywhere. I came around the bend in the road and there they were. The old teepee structures my people used to live in before axes were available. I could see how each family found the straightest poplar trees early in the spring and cut them to just the right size, using hot rocks, or burning them with fire. Then they piled the prepared trees to dry throughout the summer. Come fall when it started to cool off, the people could erect their winter homes. They would take the dried poles and build a teepee-like structure. The thin and thick ends would be alternated to make a tight fit. Wherever there was a hole it would be plugged with rawhide and sinew. An opening would be left at the top of the teepee. This would be covered by thick hide and tied tight with sinew. As I sat there looking at the fallen poles, I could see everything in my mind.

When it started to cool off in the fall, rocks were heated to white hot on a fire outside and brought in to keep the teepees warm throughout the night. Almost all the cooking was done outside the teepee, but when the cold winter winds began to howl and the temperatures dropped well below zero, it was necessary to move inside. When people needed to make a fire, they would pull the top flaps back, so the smoke could escape. Mostly they burned birch wood as it does not make sparks like some of the hardwoods. It also burns cleaner and produces the most heat. In my youth back at Lubicon Lake I remembered the lifestyle we lived, but we did have axes, so it was much easier.

I remembered the old ones talking about how they would make soup before we got pots and pans from the Bay. Holes were made in the ground and lined it with a hide. Water would be put in the lined hole. Rocks were heated until they were white hot and placed in the water. That way the water would be heated for soup, or tea. Sometimes meat would be cooked on top of the hot rocks. As I stood there, I could just see my ancestors doing that. They sure knew what they were doing in those days. We're still here, so they must have done something right. I stayed for some time.

One day I was sitting by the fire, and I knew I had made some major changes. I realized that my mind was open to receiving emotionally and I felt great, my spirit soared. I remember the words of the elders. There are many lessons learned in different ways. When one hears their truth, it can be like a knife in the heart. Therefore, some may bring to the elder tobacco in one hand and a knife in the other with the words: "Grandfather, you have much to tell that will cut like this knife that I give you as a gift. I give you this tobacco and ask you to speak for me so I may find my center. I thank you and I shall listen with a prayer in my heart, that I may be calm and collected as you speak." The elder would then pray for guidance from the divine. If one is reverently seeking guidance and truth the messages will come. A true elder would receive the direction the seeker must take in his life in order to find the peace and self-worth to move on. I knew right then and there that I was ready to learn no matter what it took, and I felt good about it.

When I felt good, I could think good when I thought good, I felt good. I just knew I could learn from any situation if I just allowed myself the openness. I understood that there is always a lesson in everything. I was so excited to begin a new chapter in my life.

I thought about how, in a way, we were all pilgrims of life, each on a journey. Some people stopped here and there to chat and learn from fellow pilgrims. Some of us travel at a slow, steady pace, others move at a very fast pace. Some will take the slower people by the hand and encourage them to move forward with great caring. Some will try to drag you back and drain you of your energies. At times some just want to give up when life gets too hard. I began to see that everyone has merit. Everyone who has the desire can learn when there is true sharing and friendship. Some people and situations tested my inner and outer discipline. Now I was beginning to see that I could actually grow stronger from mistreatment. That conclusion has been proven correct many times in my earth journey. It certainly gave me a lot of food for thought as I packed up and moved on.

Right then and there I saw a lot in my mind's eye. I remembered a talk I had earlier with an elder.

I was beginning to understand that learning and growth are accomplished through life experiences, especially hardships and suffering. I began to understand that the suffering I experienced in my body, mind, heart, and spirit throughout my years in residential school and my raging years had some meaning. That made my life forward less of a struggle. I could see how those experiences helped me understand the newcomers better and appreciate what we had before contact. I began to accept that my world had changed and life after contact would be different than life before contact. Continuing on a path of anger and resentment got me or any of my people nowhere. I knew I wanted to be a positive influence and help my lost people find a way to thrive with this new reality.

I was so grateful for the time I spent with each and every elder and how they all had a big influence on my healing, my gathering of knowledge, my newfound self. When I spent the time to be respectful of the gift of the food I received and gave thanks to the Great Spirit, Mother Earth and the animal, fish, bird or plant, and they in turn would teach me as well. When I became more conscious of these teachings, I spent less time thinking about all the pain of my past. I made it a habit to smudge and pray every day. Not necessarily to even ask for things, even though I could, but also to just give thanks for everything that sustained me from day to day.

The elders often sat with those, like me, who wanted to learn in earnest. So many things I learned in those years could only be learned by watching and listening and paying attention to the teachings of the children, the elders, and all our teachers from nature. One day I realized that I had no more room for the rage I carried before. I really had purged all my hatred and my rage. Now I was able to move on and do some good things with my life. The sun shone, the grass grew, and the rivers flowed. I saw the good in it all. That day I gave thanks for all the guidance I had received from the Creator, for the Elders who had seen the vision and helped me get to where I was. That day life was good. I just got in my truck and drove off. I didn't know where I was going, but I knew everything would be much better from here on in.

Symphony of nature

In my travels I stayed outdoors a lot and one thing I began to appreciate to help me balance my soul mist was the sounds of nature. I began to pay attention with my spiritual or subconscious mind as I would take in all sounds of nature. I began calling it a symphony as there were as many sounds as in an orchestra. When I paid attention, I found those sounds were so soothing for my troubled soul. That helped tremendously to quiet my mind when it began to race too fast. I needed all the help I could get, and nature's melodies helped me gain an inner peace, an inner harmony. When I could attain that harmony, there was a sense of oneness with all Creator's creation. When I would be one with all Creation, that would give me a sense of belonging. It was like being wrapped in a nice security blanket. That state of connectedness is like being on a high on life. There is no need for alcohol or drugs to get a high. I could get it from being one with the sounds and the rhythm of the natural world.

I especially liked to be around water. It has so many sounds, each one soothing for the soul. I would sometimes sit beside a small stream and watch and listen to the sound of water gurgling across the rocks and in between the grass. It is such fun to watch the little wildlife that depended on that water. Even the insects made a sound as they buzzed here and there. The small birds would fly from tree to bush to the ground. They didn't seem to mind me there in my stillness. The plants that grew close to the stream all had a fragrance of their own. With the sounds and the smell and all the activity that surrounded the area, all was at peace. Here there was no conflict. Nature was so marvelous in its connectedness and when I sat by that stream, I would become a part of everything around me.

Sometimes when I could find a waterfall, I liked to get close and just bask in the mist, as it too was so cleansing. It too had a smell of its own as it would pick up the aroma of the vegetation as it flowed toward the falls. My little brown body loved to be cleansed by that mist.

When it rained, I loved to sit and listen to the drip drip from the trees as it nourished the plants below. I would put on my raingear and gumboots and just find a quiet place to stand or sit. I would marvel at how a raindrop would shape itself on a leaf and then trickle down toward the ground. Different little bugs would also come out to enjoy the rain. It may make such a quiet sound that the ear may not hear it, but it was heard by my spirit. The elders talked about that, and I could feel it when I became very still.

How I loved the storms as well! When the thunder beings and the lightning came and cleansed the air and the earth, it was indeed a gift to be in their presence. They too contribute to the sounds and the balance of nature. When the thunder beings left, the birds and the insects again began to move and bring back their sounds. It was so good.

I was taught how to predict the weather by watching and listening to nature. All these things I could learn when I left my rage behind. When once again my soul found peace, I became really sensitive to nature's music and rhythm, and I found a place for me. I knew I belonged. Not one crawler, many legged, insect flyer, finned ones, flying ones, four-legged or two-legged is out of place. Every plant, every flower, every grass, every tree, every person is here for a purpose and has its rightful universal place. Everyone has a purpose; everyone is dependent on one another. To know this was to have peace in my soul. I thought about how we are born innocent and pure. All that goodness and purity somehow gets lost when we grow older and mingle with others that have lost their way like the mean people at the residential schools. Listening to the symphony of nature once again purified my spirit, my soul. In the bush, I would be acutely aware that nature has no artificial colors, no artificial sounds, or flavours. It is a pure symphony of the universe.

As long as we have Mother Earth and the universal symphony of sounds and colors, we are a part of that symphony of balance and harmony. We have so much mind potential. We have both a conscious mind and a subconscious mind. We have intuition and a spiritual mind. We have been given life itself and each day of life is an opportunity to learn.

With forest loss, oil and gas pollution, open pit mining, smokestacks spewing pollutants into the air, garbage pit excavation and covering over nuclear waste are not only causing pollution at every level, and threatening our very spiritual selves, but they're also interfering with the universal symphony that is imperative to the very existence of the positive power of mankind. When we misplace our ability to tune in to the intuitive spiritual minds, we will lose a part of ourselves as humans.

I observed how changes occurred all the time. When all the grass in one particular area was eaten by the foraging animals they would just move on. The beavers moved a lot to adjust to the water levels, even the bugs will move if their environment is destroyed. This is all natural. When changes come too rapidly, creatures cannot make a quick adjustment and may stop reproducing. They cannot remain on this earth if changes create too much toxicity.

Once man can no longer hear or feel the universal connection, he will be lost. I am afraid we will lose to the evil when we do not have the strength, we are given by the symphony any more. We will move further away from the Christ-like state of our birth and ego will rule. Our spiritual minds, our connectedness will suffer and even die in some people. It already has.

Turtle Teachings

It is interesting to note that much of what the European scientists were discovering throughout the ages was known by traditional people for many centuries. For example, Galileo built a telescope and saw the moon and Venus for the first time. He studied the positions of the stars and moons in relation to the sun and concluded that the sun was the center of our solar system. At the time the Pope considered himself the center of the universe and suggesting otherwise was blasphemy. I guess he figured that the sun and the planets rotated around him. Anyway, Galileo was put under house arrest for the last ten years of his life for his belief.

Our people had no need to have written proof that the sun was the center of our immediate solar system, or that the earth was round. Centuries before contact we had this knowledge. We knew that there were other planets too which were round and rotated around the sun. Every tribe in North America knew that North America is Turtle Island.

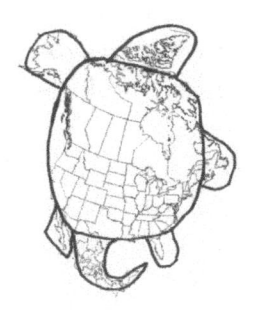

Turtle Island-North America

I do not remember the first time that the elders talked about Turtle Island. It is as if it has always been something I knew. The elders used to say that we were living on the back of the turtle. I was so young that I could not understand all they were referring to. It was only when I was older and in school that I understood that Turtle Island is all North America. Then I wondered how the elders knew that. They must have been able to fly really high in order for to see the bigger picture.

I do remember some of the turtle teachings as taught to me by the elders. All the animals taught us something. The turtle taught patience. It was so slow moving, but it always reached its goal. It was close to the ground, so it knew when things were happening on Mother Earth.

This knowledge had been passed by our wisdom keepers from generation to generation for centuries before. This may be hard to believe, but it is true. How did they know? My people were astro-travelers before they lost their power. Well, it's not totally lost. There are still those who walk this earth that have this ability, but not as many as in the old days. That is why we called the sun our father. There was Father Sun and Mother Earth. Together they sustained us for all our needs. Our wisdom keepers were great observers of our universe. The seasons came and went as the earth rotated around the sun. They even knew about the poles.

I remember how the elders would talk about how God/ Creator created the universe, the pure skies, air, clear babbling brooks, streams, rivers, lakes, and oceans and all the waters. He created the light, the sun and moon. He created our Mother the Earth, the winged ones, the finned ones, two legged ones, the four legged, the many legged ones, all just the right size and the right space for our Mother the Earth. He created all plants, small and tall. He created a fragrance for all His plant people. He gave voice and song to all moving creatures, large and small. He created a natural order of all His Creation to follow. He taught everyone to walk softly on Mother Earth. That meant that you are always to be respectful and learn what you can by watching and listening.

The turtle is also the teacher of time. The back of the turtle has 13 segments, the number of moons in a year. Surrounding the 13 segments are 28 smaller segments, the number of days in a moon cycle. That was the cycles we were taught to follow.

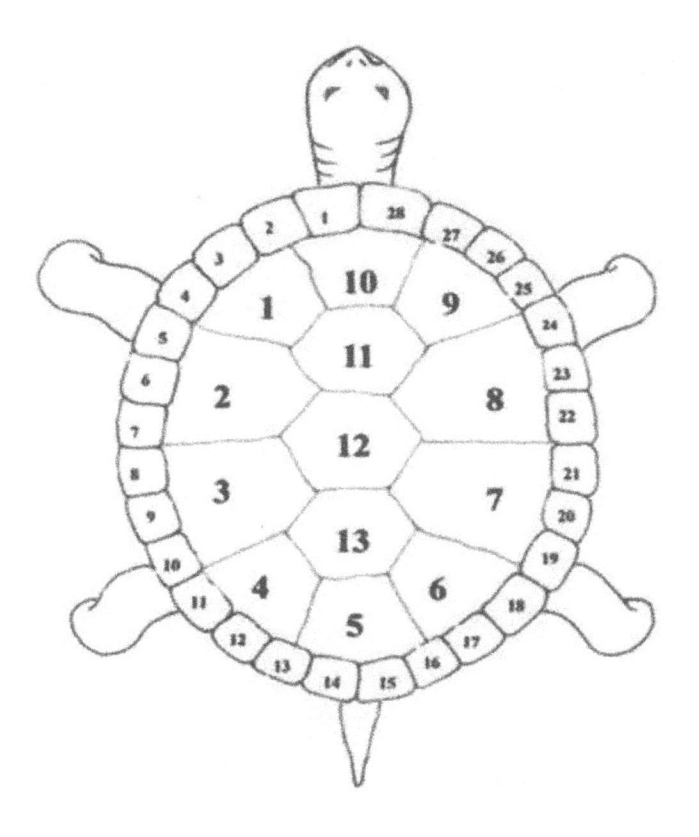

The turtle calendar

Each cycle had a special activity which we followed. There was berry picking time, hunting time. There was time for the earth to rest and a time to reawaken. Each segment has a special significance. There is a cycle for the great moon month, a cycle for the return of the eagle, a cycle named for the return of the geese, a cycle for the coming of the frogs, an egg-laying cycle, a cycle for hatching of the eggs, a molting cycle, a flying cycle, a mating cycle, migrating cycle, frosty cycle, the letting go cycle, and the going within cycle. Each cycle had special ceremonies to celebrate the changes in a year. These ceremonies I cannot share. They are not for writing. All the celebrations of the moons on Turtle Island vary

119

a little from tribe to tribe, but all have their ceremonies, their stories. This was our calendar. We knew our moon cycles and we knew our days by how much of the moon showed itself. We knew the time of day by using hand signals as to the placement of the sun. We knew where to meet using a description of landmarks. We had the where and the when for all our gatherings. We knew what we were doing. It's no wonder the European people are not well. They have lost track of the natural life cycles and adopted man-made ways of keeping track of time.

Sundance

Following is information, which some will disagree with me sharing even such a little bit of it all, but it is time we share what we know. We have kept it a secret long enough. Many people would be better off if they knew about and experienced sacredness. The time is here. I know this.

I knew I had more to learn, and I wanted more time with the elders. I would seek them out where the ceremonies were held, and I attended all I could. The message from elders, over and over again, was to stop looking for my soul everywhere else and come back to myself and be WHO I am. I don't think I understood down deep what they really meant. I guess I was not ready. I could not stay in one place for long. In my wandering I started going to sundances.

The sundance is the biggest ceremony of the year. Preparation for the sundance begins with ceremonies in February and ends with putting up the big lodge in June, July and even in August. From start to finish people go to the sundance maker for help. Only the elders who are so gifted could put up the sundance. This all was so physically demanding that they would have to stay focused all the way through. Only a man could carry this load. This would be a man who has walked the path of the ancients and has been honored with such an important role. This task is only taken on through divine revelation, as in a vision, or may be passed on from another master that is near departure from physical life. This is like one deserving person is passing on their gifts to another deserving person. It is most likely that the chosen person is one of the elder's helpers. They likely have had years of experience in that most sacred lodge.

People arrive from near and far on the designated Thursday called camping day. The last of a series of ceremonies called singings, which began in February, are celebrated and the big sundance lodge is built by the helpers the next day.

It is a most sacred time when people fast. There is drumming and singing and dancing, praying, and naming ceremonies and more. People gather for spiritual learning, to be healed and to socialize at this most sacred time.

It takes many people to put up the lodge. There is so much work to be done. Everything is done in a prayerful state. The helpers all know that it is a requirement, and they work accordingly. When I first began to work as a helper, I became a part of a team, or unit; we all had to work without being told or reminded. I would observe others and pitch in where I could. We worked with joy and we never forgot to tell stories and have a good laugh. It was good for my soul to know I was a part of a team that did such sacred work. I felt very honored to be able to work as a helper. It was a time and place where I was at peace in my soul as I listened and learned.

Many people set up camp in a large circle surrounding the big lodge. The last of the series of ceremonies which began in February are celebrated. Everyone enters the lodge with more ceremony when it is time. Until Sunday afternoon, there is drumming and singing and dancing, praying, and naming ceremonies.

One time when I was at a sundance and a beautiful girl came, the elder caught me eying her in a sexual manner. That elder gave me 'the look' and I knew I had done wrong. He didn't say a word, but I could see and feel his disapproval and I knew that I had screwed up. I immediately returned to the task at hand. I was so embarrassed and that day I learned my lesson about staying pure in ceremonies. I will never forget it. Had he not corrected my conduct, or had I not adjusted my behaviour and thought, I would not have been passed any wisdom at that ceremony.

When the sundance was over, everyone had to leave the grounds taking everything away that they had brought in. Then nature would take care of the rest. I walked away without looking back.

After the sundances were over I would just jump in my truck and move on. I started dropping in on elders whenever I could. Getting back to that wisdom I was born with took much work and sacrifice. In our modern world many have cluttered their lives with what someone else has told them as to what and how to think, instead of taking the time to go inside themselves.

In order to recover my inner self, I did a lot of meditation, fasting and ceremonies. I sat many hours with the wisdom keepers. Slowly my life turned around. I was becoming more settled in my heart, my spirit. I was becoming stronger as I began to know the person I really was born to be.

As a free thinker, I began seeing the world with more clarity. I concluded that there was no peace in the teachings of the white schools, churches, political and legal systems, or in their society in general. I also saw much clearer the reality of our situation as Native people in Canada. If we were to survive, we needed to do so within the parameters of cooperation with the new reality of colonization by the newcomers. That has been a challenge for my people ever since contact and still is today. We all question how much we can work together and what we can sacrifice and what we cannot. If my people were to survive at all, we would have to learn the newcomer's ways, their language and their way of looking at the world. I could never agree with them, but I could learn to negotiate with them. I would need to stand on their rock. I held onto the fact that I could always go back to the bush. I could still hunt and live with nature, with the Creator and Mother Earth. When I needed strength, I could find it in the bush.

The realization that I could work both worlds gave me a lot of strength for what I knew would be a difficult journey. I began to formulate a plan to help others to purge themselves of the pain of colonization and teach how to take advantage of what the newcomers brought and still not give up what we have. I realized we had no choice but to live in both worlds if we were to survive at all.

I was finally, for the first time since residential school, able to take my freedom to explore inside. Sometimes I spent a week or two in the bush by myself. I would pitch a tent and go to sleep every night to the sounds of nature. A lot of time was spent sitting by a bonfire and connecting with all things around me. There I was free to think, to learn the ways of nature, to connect with Creator, and to my inner self.

I wandered restlessly as I needed to spend time alone in order to have time to contemplate on how I live my future. I knew I had more work to do as I did not feel truly in balance and I knew I would need all my strength to continue my earth journey in an effective and productive way. By this time my body was doing well, but my mind, heart, and spirit still needed a little help. I was doing much better with the understanding of my weaknesses, but I still needed to always be aware of fully embracing positive thinking. That is a huge challenge. None of us are perfect, but I try.

I spent more time with elders in my hunger for knowledge. These elders taught me how to make the most of my gifts and challenges, but it was only in my solitude that I could fully absorb all this profound knowledge. The elders helped bring back my self-esteem and self-worth. I talked to myself a lot as I drove my old Ford truck from one community to the next, and I realized that I had the gift of words, or maybe it was just the gift of the gab. I slowly made adjustments in my attitude for a better life. I continued to work toward becoming all I could be. I began to see that I could make myself useful in this world.

I discovered I had a singing voice. Once I met up with a friend – I can't remember his name. He had a guitar, and I was immediately attracted to the sound. I didn't have money for a guitar, but I went back to my village and found some old wires from an old bed stead. I found a square tin can and made a guitar out of it. Didn't work very well so I went to the Bay and got some guitar strings and made my own guitar out of cardboard. It worked better.

One day a group of friends got together and formed a band called 'The Flickers.' Then I bought a real good-looking guitar which cost me two dollars. Once it got wet and I found out that it too was made of cardboard. Later I did get a real guitar made out of wood. It was my pride and joy. The band was headed up by Bill Willier and I joined shortly after it was formed. I was the lead singer. We travelled from community to community and played for weddings, anniversaries, graduations, and all kinds of events. We really had fun with that band, telling jokes and making witty remarks about people. We loved to play tricks on people, especially the RCMP. One of our favorites was to short-circuit the fanciest car we could see in a hotel parking lot, and drive it four or five blocks away and then short-circuit another car and drive it back. We just wanted to get one over on the big shots and the police. It's a wonder we never got caught. Another thing we did was build the first PA system we ever saw. It served us well to increase the volume of our music. We made it out of an old radio. Although it was scratchy, it worked. Those were good times. CKYL radio station in Peace River used to run a search for talent program. I decided to try out and I got a spot. I ended up winning in Peace River and the next step was to go to Camrose for a provincial run-off. The person who came in second was so unhappy and thought he should have won, so I gave him my spot. I felt myself getting stronger and stronger in the time I spent with the band, but I once again got restless, so I moved on.

As I travelled, I taught myself much. My search for knowledge took over for the raging and pain and agony which had consumed my life earlier. Sitting and observing the birds, the trees, and even the bugs brought new knowledge every day. In fact, some call the bugs the little Gods. I could see how every creature had a place in the bigger picture of this our Earth.

Researching became my new life. I worked hard to become a good reader and studied how to use the English words in the English way. I found out what our legal rights were or weren't. Now I could function in both worlds. Throughout the years my hard work has paid off. No one could fool me.

I began to understand clearly many of the consequences of the changes that had infiltrated our world. For instance, in the old days our families were small, but, after residential school, women started to have more and more children because too many followed the Catholic teachings of no birth control. Today it is proven that uneducated people had the most children. Just one more reason for increasing education levels.

In my wanderings I attended many conferences. Everything was more learning, more time spent with a large variety of people. Billy Thomas, my relation, was always a good storyteller. Billy Thomas was born into the old tradition as well. He went to an Anglican Residential school close to his home. He was allowed to go home every weekend, so he never lost the traditional language or way of life. Not like the people who went to the Grouard Residential School. They stayed all through the school year and most were abused. The people who were allowed to go to Lubicon Lake School were mostly treated with dignity and respect. Billy Thomas and Billy Joe Laboucan, amongst others, maintained the sense of humour and storytelling skills of our people. They liked to pull a fast one on everyone. One time I was at an elders' conference and Billy Thomas told this story. "Henry Laboucan was a fearless warrior who proudly rode horses into the opponent's territory. He was one with his horse and paid little attention to anything else. He didn't even notice that he had dropped his loin cloth and was chasing the other tribesmen in the nude. Today Henry is still looking for his loin cloth." It was a time of good fellowship and good sharing and good strategizing.

One time I travelled north on the Peace River. Not far from Garden River was a little red house and church. An old man named Charlie Wapus lived there. "Come with me," he told me. He took me to a village which had been there for at least 200 years. Charlie had insight into the battle of the Dog Ribs long before it happened. I would call him a 'seer.' He showed me the place where the battle between the Cree and the Dogrib happened. We found a muzzle-loader gun and a pipe which was left behind by the Dogrib people. It is sad it came to this.

In 1991 I was travelling aimlessly in my old truck pulling an old camper which I had picked up earlier. It was certainly a step up from sleeping in my truck. I travelled down a dirt road north of Slave Lake. Suddenly I came across a bunch of teepees and decided to pull in to see what was happening. As it turned out Raven Makkannaw and Madge McRee were sponsoring an RCMP cultural camp. Police officers from across northern Alberta attended. There has always been a lot of friction between the police and the Native Community. This was the Police force's way of bringing the communities together, so both sides could get to know one another. Madge asked if I would like to do a presentation. As my special gift is the gift of gab, I was very happy to oblige. I gave the participants the teaching about the cycle of life and how we believe that the life journey is circular with the newborn and the old being closest to Creator. That is different from the western linear way of thinking. Later there was to be a sweat lodge and Raven gave me tobacco for the first time to run a sweat. I wondered how he knew that I was able to do that, but then the true elders just know.

Later Raven asked me to help out with the Aboriginal Diabetes Wellness program. This was a program set up in Edmonton by Capital Health. Part of the program was teaching about the traditional world view and how we could utilize the old teachings and the western medicine for a better outcome for those who were struggling with keeping their blood sugars under control. It was nice to have the opportunity to share the teachings which I had learned in all the years of sitting with the elders. At that time, I mostly stayed in Edmonton anyway. I had moved in to be near my sister who was gravely ill.

One time we were out in the bush in a cultural camp by Marten River. The late Madge McRee was there teaching about the woman stuff. Raven Makkannaw was also teaching in that camp. Madge asked to have her grandchild lifted up as in the old days. First of all, a pipe was smoked for a blessing for the new little life which had just come into the world. Then the child was passed from one elder to the next who held the child as high toward the sky as they could. Everyone said a special prayer for that child and committed to being there for teachings and health. It was very special to have been a part of that.

My travels also brought me to Seabird Island, a reserve close to Mission in BC. They had a gathering in the longhouse. I was lucky enough to participate in a traditional ceremony of figuring out how to recreate harmony where disharmony had crept in. A couple who were cheating on each other, were called to face the people that were cheated on. They also had to face their community in their shame. The couple that was cheated on had the opportunity to have their say about how it affected them. I cannot go into detail as that is very private. I can tell you that everyone affected had their say in front of the community and each other. The elders spent much time talking about the harm that was done and made suggestions as to how everyone could proceed. In the end it was up to the injured parties to make their own decision. This was so close to the way we did it back home. It was good for my soul to see that others were still practicing the old ways, which are just as relevant and efficient as ever.

In 2011 I was helping the Cardinal family facilitate a fast and many people were in attendance. Among them was a friend of a friend from Denmark, Claus Marquart Jorgensen. He passed me one of my most treasured possessions: a bracelet with Nelson Mandella's prison number on.

I have always had a great affinity for Nelson, as there were many parallels in the experience of his people and mine. In fact, we still have what we call our own Nelson Mandella in Leonard Peltier. He, as Nelson, was fighting for the freedom of his people when he was falsely accused of gunning down two FBI officers. The fear of our people is that Leonard will die in jail. Nelson is free and we pray that Leonard will also one day see the 'outside.'

In 2014 a large contingent of people attended a gathering in Ft. Chip, as everyone calls it. Ft. Chip is located on the northeast tip of Lake Athabasca. It is about 200 km. north of Ft. McMurray.

There were approximately 160 people present at the gathering. About eight elders got very weak and felt ill so they had to rush home. I actually started to shake myself and had to leave. I think the people of Ft. Chip have gotten so used to the pollution from the tar sands that they did not get as sick as the rest of us who came from the 'outside.' Too bad no one listened to the elders in the first place. The wisdom keepers knew that the big oil companies were doing too much too fast. No one opposed development but wanted it done in an environmentally friendly way.

I heard there was a conference at the Coast Terrace Inn in Edmonton, so I thought I would head down to Edmonton and see for myself. There was nothing going on there, so I got back in my suburban, which I was driving at that time. My instincts told me to head south, and I ended up in Devon. I knew it was not here I should stop, so I continued driving until I got to Rocky Mountain House, 190 km away. I met up with some buddies there, and we all decided to enter the fastball competition under the name of the Wabasca Athletics, and we won. During that tournament I, for the first time, really looked at the white guys and discovered there were some things that were at least bearable as fellow ball players. That was a big step forward for me.

In my travels I have always been lucky enough to pick up enough work to keep me and my truck going. I was always told by the elders that when you really need money it will come, and it always did. I just had to keep the faith.

I often drove aimlessly, and I was free to think and evaluate my past and my present. I am happy to have grown up a Bush Cree. I remembered sitting with the elders when I was young – before being kidnapped and sent to residential school. Remembering their teachings and their stories made my journeys in my truck downright enjoyable. I would stop sometimes, build a fire and make myself a cup of tea. Then I would sit quietly with my memories and now I knew I could think of a better future. I would contemplate on what the real meaning behind the elder's stories were. I would often sit for a long time as I concentrated on every word relayed so long ago.

Soon I would become one with the trees, the fire and all nature around me. That was when I would get a deeper understanding of the teachings. The elders did not exaggerate or expound their own ideas. When they taught the old ways, they followed their teacher's words to the letter and honoured the source of their knowledge.

Sometimes I was only given just enough information to know I would have to find my own answers. This is deep shshtuff. The elders might talk about what I could learn from certain plants, but I also had to learn how to approach the plants according to protocol. I would have to gift Creator, Mother Earth and the plant with tobacco and prayers of gratitude and ask for whatever I wanted to learn. When I sat with a plant long enough in a meditative state, the teachings would most likely come. That is why I say that some teachings could only be learned by experience. I would then go back to my teachers, and we would talk. He or she would confirm my conclusions or not.

In the beginning I thought I could learn quite well by taking shortcuts, such as shortening my time in ceremony, or a fast, or meditation time. There was also very strict protocol about keeping my mind off women at sacred times. Later I realized that the elders did have my best interests at heart when they made me stay from start to finish.

One day I attended an elders' conference in Peace River. Everyone shared about how to live a better life. One elder spoke about light and darkness: "Darkness does not understand the light and is therefore afraid of the light. They will attack what they do not understand. All we can do is pray for those people who remain in darkness, that they might one day come to understand the goodness and the teachings of the light."

Others shared about how a person must learn to walk on their own in balance and harmony. Only when the negativity is dealt with, will your intuition and instinct become guiding forces you can tap into. All humans are given these gifts, but too many discards them when the negative forces take over their lives. There are many barriers I had to overcome. So much to learn. Being in the presence of the old helped to quench my thirst for knowledge. The ability to utilize instinct and intuition needs to be retrieved if we have forgotten it in our cluttered world. Children have it. We are born with it. Then we have to re-remember. You must be healthy in every way in order to be passed the spiritual wisdom.

Willie Hamelin

One day I was called to Grouard to Willie Hamelin's side. He was getting ready to leave this earth. He asked everyone else to leave the room as he wanted to have a personal talk with me.

It was Willie that used to pick us up and take us away to residential school. He had to split families and send them to different places. Even as far away as Joussard and all the way to Hay River in the Northwest Territories. I really felt that he was asking for forgiveness for what he did. There is a language of the heart. He did not have to explain. As I sat there by his side as he lay dying, we didn't say much. We didn't need to. We both knew each other's thoughts. Then he handed me the poster called the destiny manifesto. He told me, "You will know what to do with this. Some day you will be talking about it," he said as he handed me one of the few remaining posters. Most have been destroyed. I felt he was asking my forgiveness for his role within the church. I did forgive him. He died shortly after. This was in 1974, I think, or thereabouts.

Part 6
Professional Life

Affirmative Action Program

My wanderings in the late 1960s gave me a lot of time to think about what was needed for my people. We were the Earth keepers and now invaders had arrived and taken over Turtle Island our Mother, the Earth, and we were powerless to stop it.

We the Earth keepers had been manhandled into silence for too long. I realized we had to deal with this new reality in order to receive recognition and opportunities to work in the 'white' world. I decided to take a course as a life skills coach. Although I knew more about what they were teaching than the instructors, I knew I had to do as I was told in order to get their certification. When I graduated, I just jumped in the truck and away I went.

When the first European people came, they were welcomed into our community. Some traders were open to learn, and we all gained a lot from each other. Some learned our language and they helped us to learn English. It was from them we learned that all white people were not mean, were not like the police, the politicians and the priests and nuns. For many of my people they were the only positive influence from the newcomers.

One advantage we saw was the importance of having our children integrated into the public-school system as they would then have the same opportunities for education as the white kids. There were other problems with that however as by that time there was an inherent belief within the public-school system that Native kids were just not as smart as their white counterparts. When you are only six years old a teacher has a great influence on you. To this day that is presenting challenges for our young students.

I saw the results of what happened to the young people who were kidnapped and punished for being 'Indian,' for speaking their language, for saying their prayers, and for the loneliness which too often broke their spirits. It all took its toll. Alcohol was never a part of our culture, but our people drank mainly to kill the pain of what happened. When they were torn away from all the teachings of their parents and elders, and from the love of their community and from the teachings with kindness, which was the way of the old ones, too many became broken. By the time the priests and nuns were done with them, innocence and confidence was no more. Our people had been whipped into behaving and thinking in the European way, so in the end they ended up not belonging anywhere. Pain, anger, frustration and dealing with deceitful people was our destiny. We see today where that legacy has been passed down from one generation to the next. I know, because I strayed from the original teachings myself and lived some years in the darkness. I am not proud of what I did, but I guess it was something I had to go through.

In 1939, the Indian Association of Alberta was formed with individual membership, rather than bands. Harold Cardinal, from the Sucker Creek reserve in northern Alberta, had completed his Doctor of Law degree in 1968 at age twenty-three. He was voted in as president of the Indian Association of Alberta. He understood the Canadian legal system and the treaties.

Down south, in what now is called the USA, wars were going on for a long time between the new-comers and first nations. That is how they dealt with claiming land. That was not the way it was done here. Land sharing in Canada was resolved with treaties that first nations signed with the Dominion of Canada. A treaty is an agreement, a contract or a truce, between two or more sovereign states according to international law. Our thinking at the time was that the treaties had benefits for our communities and were intended to foster good relations between ourselves, the Crown and all people in Canada. Through the treaties we were giving the newcomers permission to share our land and sharing was very much a part of our culture. We were so misled. The treaties have been broken time and again. Harold helped us to understand how to interpret them.

I heard some communities were uniting in the north with the vision of making a difference for our people in this new world. I decided to check it out. Much of the treaty 8 area constituted small communities. Harold Cardinal helped us to understand how we could use the Canadian laws to our advantage. He envisioned the struggle ahead as he fought hard to assure that, in his words, "We have the right to be the red tile in the Canadian mosaic."

As president of the Indian Association, Harold Cardinal spent time with the Euro/Canadian politicians and he would share with the people what we had to do in order to become involved on a political level, where we needed a voice in order to move ahead in this new reality we faced. We had to learn how to talk to the government. With guidance from Harold these communities came to realize that they would have more political power with the government if they united. Therefore, they formed the Isolated Communities Association. It consisted of seven communities including Peerless Lake, Trout Lake, Lubicon Lake, Chipewyan, Sandy Lake, Loon Lake and Cadotte Lake.

Only the Lubicon had a land claim which had not yet been settled, even after all these years. Our band at Lubicon Lake did not have a treaty to share our land with the newcomers. When the Canadian official who travelled up in our area signed treaties to the left and to the right, but for some reason forgot about that bush area in the middle. With those harsh winters and no roads, and only trees to be seen, there probably was not much of value in their eyes. That is how our land slipped through their fingers.

The others were granted reserves. The main leaders were Henry Noskey, William Noskey, Fred Noskey, William Beaver and Edward Sinclair. It was recognized by that group that there was a great need for western education. They also worked hard to get better health facilities and addressed land claims and broken treaties and more. We did a lot of strategizing hoping that someone who had the power to make changes would listen. The government did and we got funding. We set up the Affirmative Action Program to improve the education standard. William Beaver and Edward Sinclair were the leaders. I became the field supervisor. The vision was to educate the people to become teachers and lawyers and politicians and business owners. We saw it was the way of the future.

We wanted our students to understand about human nature and what had happened to them so they could recognize where they were and where they could get to. We wanted to give our people hope for their future by bringing them back to their culture and at the same time teach the western training to survive in our new reality.

Traditional living skills and traditional teachings had to be included to repair the damage done. It was like our people were frozen in time. Individually prescribed instruction was imperative. The theme we decided on was 'recovering our spirit.' We used numerous circle teachings to bring the students into the circle of connectedness. Then they could very quickly pick up the western education. In 1980 AVC set up a campus in Grouard. They offered the Education Technicians program that taught my people how to teach the western portion of our program. Now we had it all and it was good.

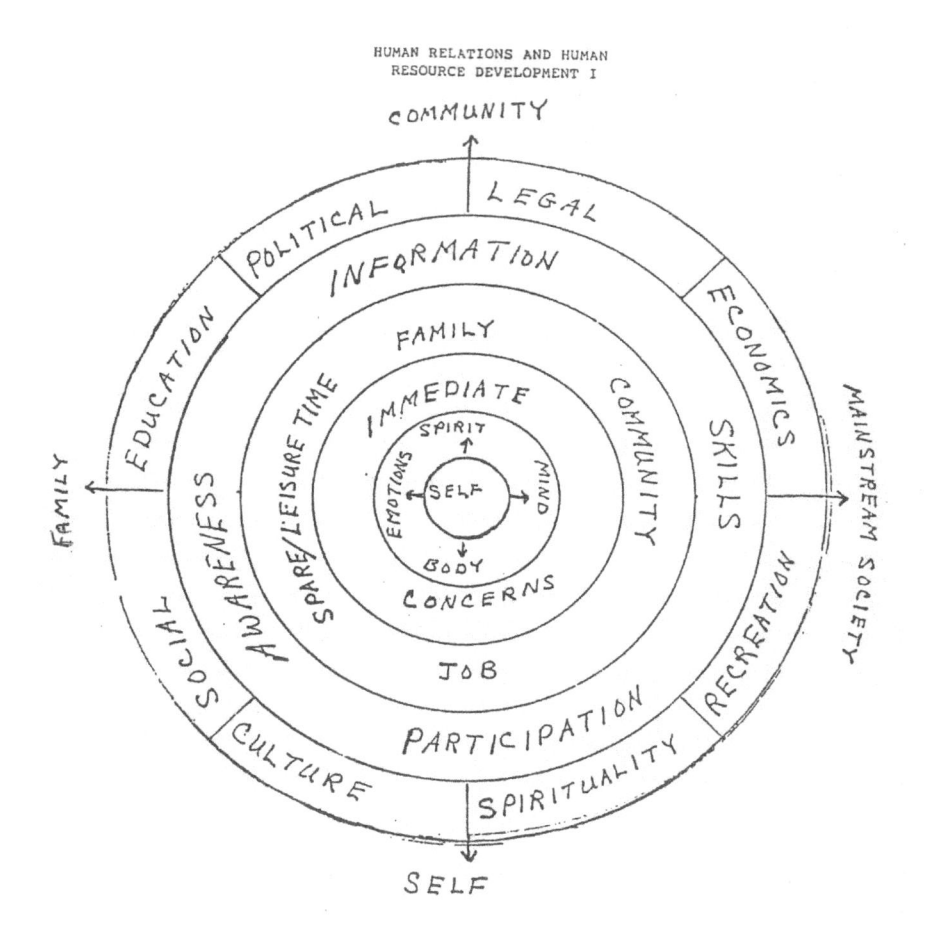

An example of the use of the circle for life skills teaching.

My role in this was to travel all throughout northern Alberta and convince our people of the benefits of getting a western education, along with reclaiming

WHO they were as proud Neheyowuk (Cree people). To that extent I spent much time on the road as each village was far from the next, and there were no modern amenities. Sometimes I would stop by the side of the road and cook a meal or make a cup of tea. I travelled 27,000 miles over small, dusty bush roads to find suitable locations. There was no pavement back then. The roads were full of ruts and when it rained it would become quite a challenge to stay between the ditches. When I dropped in on people, they would never send me away without food, so I always had some dry meat and bannock. Enough to keep me going.

The residential school had been shut down, since 1962, but the building still stood. We decided that would be a good central location to start. It did have its drawbacks as countless people were hurt so deeply there. That became my challenge. To help the people realize the importance of education and to convince them that they could overcome the harm done. The fact that it was run by Aboriginal people did persuade them to return. As transportation between northern communities was a challenge, we realized we needed small campuses all over the northern region.

Whenever I could get radio coverage, I would sing along to songs played on CFRN out of Peace River. My favorites were Marty Robbins and Hank Williams. I also liked Kitty Wells, Elvis Presley and Johnny Cash, but they were not my favorites, so I would listen to them with less intensity. They were just background noise. Over a year was spent getting these facilities set up and looking for teachers for each one. Sometimes I would stay with friends, but I also spent nights sleeping in my truck. I always carried my guitar with me and wherever a few people would gather we would sing and dance and have fun. It was hard work, but worth it.

We managed to set up satellite centers at High Level, Ft. Vermillion, Assumption, Meander River, Paddle Prairie, Manning, Valleyview, Sturgeon Lake, Green Court, High Prairie, Sucker Creek, Trout Lake, Atikemeg, Gift Lake, Joussard, Faust, Kinuso, Driftpile reserve, Slave Lake, Wabasca, Chipewyan Lake, Calling Lake, Sandy Lake, Smith, Cadotte Lake, Loon Lake and Lubicon Lake. We rented or purchased facilities wherever we could. Most had no running water or indoor plumbing, but we kept going the best we could. Some stayed open longer than others.

After some basic life skills teachings, we needed upgrading from 1-7. In residential school we were only taught to about a grade 2 level, even though we went there for so many years. We were told we could only do dirt work anyway. We did not have the intelligence for more. We knew our people were smart enough to do anything and we wanted to provide the opportunity. We did get programs, not only for upgrading, but for business administration, corporate business training, health careers, humanity services, trades and technology and University preparation. Our teachers were often just only one step ahead of the pupils, but we did it. We based our program on how the black people in the States first made the transition from slavery to freedom. This one would be for Aboriginal people by Aboriginal people. The traditional teachings promoted pride in who they were as young Cree men and women, and they developed the mindset that the sky is the limit.

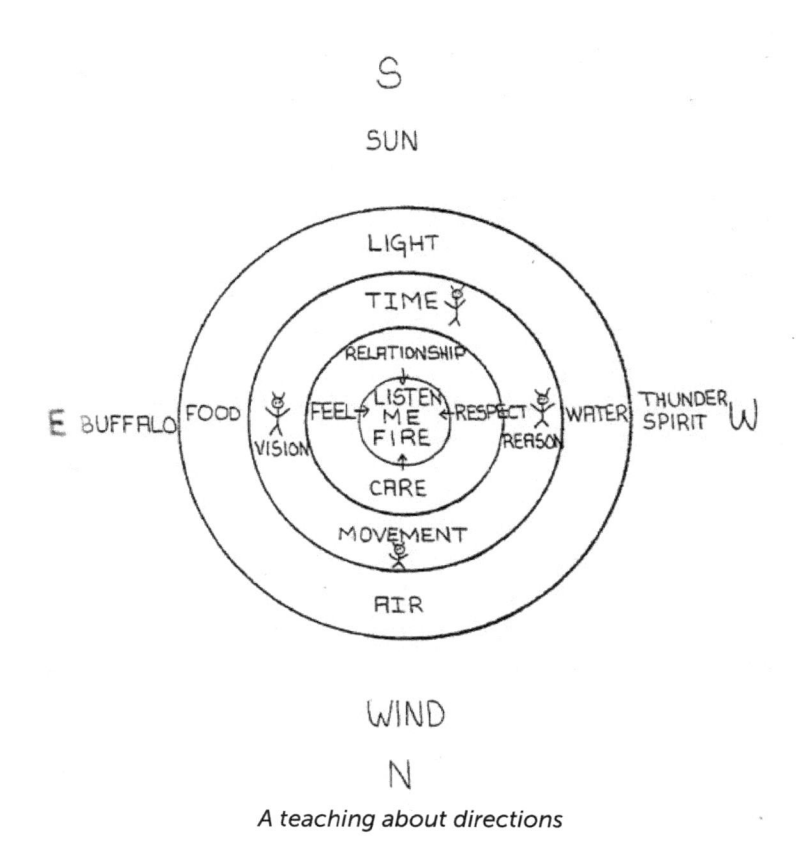

A teaching about directions

You may wonder why South is at the top of the circle and North at the bottom. The earth is a sphere, so up and down depends on how you view the world. For us we always said down north as water runs down and water ran north. Made sense to us.

Universal Clock

The Great Sacred Circle

THE LIGHT
(GOD / UNIVERSE) PERFECTION

SUN

ENLIGHTENMENT — Away From The Light
MOVING TO DARKNESS

DAWN ← MOTHER EARTH → DUSK

MOVING TO THE LIGHT

NIGHT
- IN DARKNESS
- LOWEST LEVEL OF BEING

GETTING AWAY FROM
- GOD CONSCIOUSNESS
- UNIVERSE CONSCIOUSNESS
- UNIVERSE INTELLIGENCE
- MORALS, VALUES, ETHICS
- Christstate, MasterState
- Our Birthright

OR

UNIVERSAL CLOCK

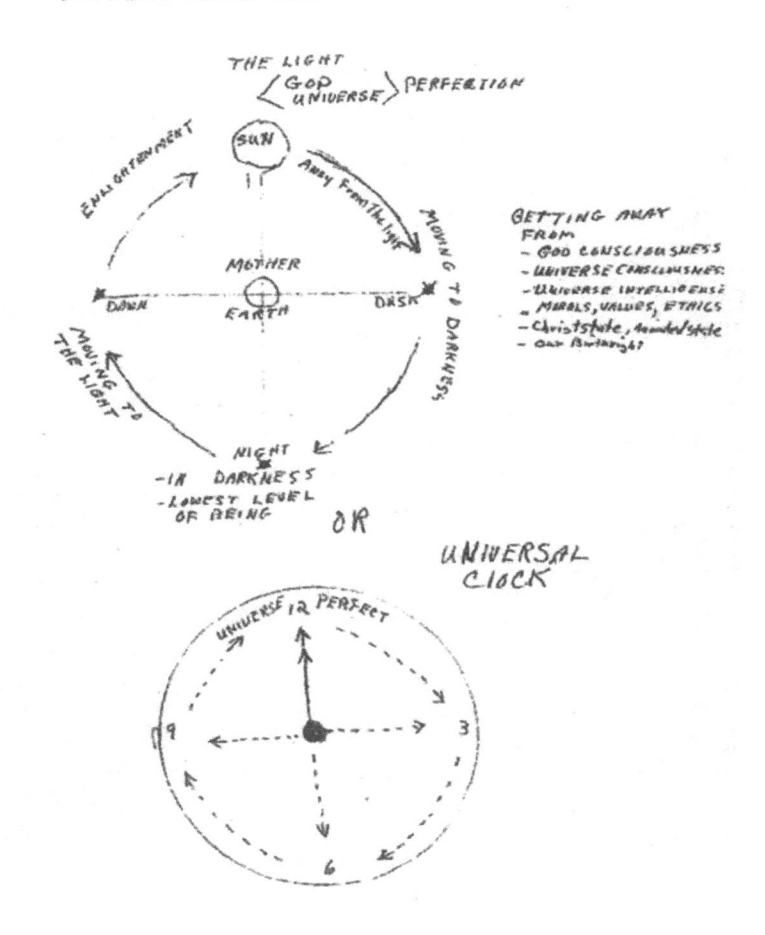

UNIVERSE IS PERFECT

12 / 3 / 6 / 9

Recognizing where a person was at and how they could move on.

We taught the students to recognize where they were at by using the universal clock teachings.

One of the teachings was that a person who is angry, has low self-esteem, low levels of acceptance and tolerance might think they are able to use intuition, but they are not. Before a person can fully utilize the Creator's gifts, they must take care of body, mind and spirit. The sacred guidance of respect, love, honesty, humbleness, courage, wisdom and truth were to be a guide to a life well lived, no matter what their vocation would become. If people abused their God-given sexual powers, if they allowed bad thoughts to enter their minds and not think with clarity, there will not be room for the good and productive messages to come through. They will not be open to receive if the spirit is not healthy.

We taught that when a person does not feel ok about something, it is a sign to figure out why they feel that way and work toward fixing it. That negative feeling is a message that changes are necessary. The uncomfortable feelings are a gift – because how else would a person know that there are better things for them? The elders would never condemn anyone who did wrong. They understood that that person needed help, not condemnation. If one meets anger with anger, what help can you be to others? When we learn to meet anger with love and caring, we have a chance to become a better people.

We wanted to move the students toward healing and balance so that they in turn spread that energy to others. Having the strength and skill to deal with emotions is a gift we wanted our students to have. We wanted to keep our people out of jail. We understood that the people who end up in our jails are mostly people who have lost their power. We knew the key was to teach traditional life skills to the people who were incarcerated so they too could regain their power and they could begin to live a good life. Our work, which we began way back then, has resulted in elders going into the jails to help inmates restore themselves to balance. The work that I did so many years ago, to make that help available to the inmates, makes me feel good, because it is good. The gifts of feeling and emotions confirm this.

In life skills we taught about how everything in nature is circular and perhaps the most sacred of all circles is the circle of life. The teaching tool we used for this is a wall clock with hour and minute hands. Mother Earth would be at the center and the sun would be at twelve o'clock. The old ones spoke of stars at the twelve o'clock, three o'clock, six o'clock and nine o'clock directions. This concept would be used to teach the movement of all change. Winter was at the 12 o'clock position, continuing into spring equinox at the three o'clock position. Summer and solstice would be at the bottom in the six o'clock position. Fall equinox would fall at nine o'clock, and then back up to winter solstice and 12 o'clock. When you draw a line between the four directions a perfect cross and balance would be the result. This would symbolize that there is perfect harmony and cooperation of the universe and a natural order on Mother Earth with all its life.

Another teaching used was that when the minute and the hour hand would line up at twelve o'clock, it would symbolize perfect alignment. Three o'clock and on symbolizes the moving away from perfect alignment and toward the darkness, and the beginning of poor attitude and behaviour. The disrespect for others, the foul language, the sexual promiscuity is a sign that those people are on their way to six o'clock. Six o'clock means a movement into total darkness, the opposite of the perfect alignment at twelve o'clock. The darkest form of mankind. At six o'clock you find the drug addicts, the murderers, the rapists, the creators of wars and all immorality. As well you will also find the dark, unnatural side of spiritualism. Here lives the demonism, the dark side of witchcraft. This is a sick place for individuals, families, towns, countries, and the world. It is from this state that hatred and wars are created. It is from this state that evil spreads.

Nine o'clock would symbolize the movement out of darkness and back to the light, the enlightenment. It represented a movement toward perfection. The best-known example of someone who stayed in that light is Jesus, who became the Christ, the anointed one, the most enlightened one.

These are the teachings of the natural laws. This is not to say that every member of every tribe actually lived this way. Some betrayed themselves on the path and moved away from the light into the darkness. As we develop our spiritual side, we will move from eight o'clock through nine, ten and eleven o'clock on the universal clock. So, our attitude and behavior are determining factors as to where one lives on the universal clock or great circle of life.

If your spirit is trying to tell you something through instinct and intuition, you may not sense or feel what is being passed if your lives are cluttered with alcohol and drugs. When the decline of following the natural laws occur, it is a move away from pure light of universal perfection. We have those God-given gifts of the seven principles to live by and guide us. These were passed to learn from, to help us grow and to guide us to a healthy and happy way of being.

We have been passed the seven power centers and the seven gifts to help us understand how we can live a good balanced life.

For those who are at nine o'clock to eleven o'clock on the universal clock, there is no need for man-made laws. The man-made laws that are supposed to discipline mankind teach us nothing about how to move to a lighter place on the universal clock. The students needed to know that they could move out of the darkness and into the light. If that happens, there is no need for discipline from others. Once one has that wisdom, they will never be able to go back to the darkness on the universal clock.

These were the teachings at the school. The old ones reminded us how important it was to remember that our own morals and values are our ethics and we had to live the good life before we could teach others.

As we look at the Great Sacred Circle of life, we see the missionaries and residential schools were living and modelling that of three o'clock to six o'clock because their behaviour was so mean and narrow and shallow. It is what they passed on to most of the residential students and persuaded some that it was what God's belief really was. No wonder so many of my people got confused in their youth and ended up very broken.

As the students moved along the universal clock, we taught them a better way to live and think. My people mostly live between eight o'clock and ten o'clock. Once a person finds himself/herself moving closer to the light of twelve o'clock, one will never again regress to the six o'clock darkness.

If you take any fruit or vegetable and squeeze it; what is on the inside is what will come to the outside. Inside is perfection and nutrition. Nature is perfect enough to sustain all life on Mother Earth. All nature creatures know that perfection because they, as we, are a part of it. No improvement necessary. It is the same with us humans. What is inside us comes out. For instance, if we are cut off in traffic, or someone tailgates, and we become angry, then we are anger on the inside. We are weak. If we are strong, love and patience would come out no matter the circumstance. We must do our best to keep our power centers in a continuous state of purity. Those who know will use these to connect with intuition and instincts. When you have clear understanding of self you can discern positive from negative in other people. Your emotions, your spiritual self, is all used to 'read' another person. If all is well with yourself, you will rarely be mistaken.

Because we are born into perfection, how is it that we become imperfect? There are many influences that may lead us the wrong way, but the perfection is what we should strive for and then we will reach the understanding of enlightenment. Then we can connect with the star people who are our guides, our teachers. With the movement into an enlightened place, all things are possible. We taught the students that you can have success in career, in family, in all that you desire to dream. Having the strength and skill to deal with emotions is a gift which everyone can learn. The choice is yours.

We passed on the eagle teachings to help the students to better understand the importance of the whole – the importance of balance and harmony in their lives. Unfortunately, some of our non-traditional people have forgotten or were not taught this basic principle. Some radical and militant people are not humble and do not know the true teachings of the eagle feather.

As part of the training, we asked businesses in High Prairie to allow practical training in their establishments with the vision that the students would see that someday they too could own their own business, or be managers, like in the bank. That was successful to a point, but discrimination was rampant, and it was a big challenge for most students. Little by little education levels went up and we eventually had some University graduates. Some got a teacher's certificate as well.

Once the students became uncluttered and understood how each person was of great value, the English school teachings were a breeze. We knew they were intelligent, but so much had stood in their way. Now they could fly.

Pearl Calahasen, one of the graduates became the longest serving female member of the Alberta Legislative Assembly. Others have also held Alberta government positions. People did regain their dignity and got an education without the need to give up WHO they are as Native people. We were on top of the world. Our hard work was paying off. We were using the old teachings to survive in this new reality, and it was working as the elders told us it would. All in all, it was a great success.

All our dreams, all our hopes for the future, everything we had worked so hard for, came crashing down one day at the stroke of a pen. The Alberta Union of Public Employees began lobbying the government for our jobs and they got them. Our Education Technician's Certification was rendered useless. Members of the union were given our jobs, even though they knew nothing about traditional teachings. It was heartbreaking for the people who were working so hard to regain their pride. It was devastating for all the northern communities, for our organization, for everyone.

The union didn't understand the importance of the cultural life skills. They could not accept the fact that we could teach to their standards. Even our great results were not enough to stop the takeover. We had brought our students back to health, as well as preparing them for a future in the new world they were facing. We lost our jobs in a time when no-one would hire Indians. We lost our credentials and once more we were told we were inferior. Some people never fully recovered from that blow and turned back to the bottle. Some of us continued in the ways of the warrior, standing tall and continuing the battle, but it was a daunting task.

Once again, the newcomers took over because they thought they knew best. Once again, they portrayed themselves as the heroes who rescued my people. We did not want rescuing, we did not need rescuing, we knew what we were doing, and we were successful. Everything was twisted to make them the heroes once again. When the government set up courses in Grouard for menial work, it was a reminder of how we were always told in residential school that we were not capable of better. We wanted our people trained for professional jobs. We had to battle for that too. We knew we were as capable as the newcomers, if only we were given a chance. Our success proved us right. Our struggles continue, but we're not giving up no matter how many obstacles are continually put in our way.

Aug 25, 1999, the Northern Lakes College launched its new name. The foundation they built it on was ours. We had to fight once again to keep their main offices in Slave Lake and Grouard. We won. Today the college is open to everyone. There is still an emphasis on attracting Native students and a number of traditional programs are offered. They currently have 25 satellite CVCs dotted across the north and employ 275 staff. Some communities are Ft. Vermillion, High Level, La Crete, Paddle Prairie, Peerless Lake Cadotte Lake, Peace River, Stony Point, Gift Lake, Atikameg, Peavine, McLennan, Grouard, High Prairie, Marten Lakes Wilderness campus, Slave Lake, Driftpile, Fox Creek, Barrhead, Athabasca and Valleyview. We are happy to see that some small part of our dream is still alive, but at the same time devastated over the loss of combining traditional life skills with education. After the takeover, the opportunity for higher education and wellness for countless numbers of my people who were broken was gone. When we tried to explain that to government and the union, they didn't listen, they didn't understand. They didn't know how to deal with broken people, they just wrote them off. Still, we have to fight. We can't give up.

After that I went to the bush to recover my own spirit. It was broken again. As I sat by the fire my auntie's words of 'kiam,' let it go, kept coming into my head. I knew I could not go back to the darkness I had lived before, but I could not figure out how to move forward either. I decided I needed some help and went on to stay with Albert Lightning for a while. I did fasts and sweat lodges and slowly I too could say 'kiam.' There was nothing I could do about it anyway. That battle was lost, and I had to accept that, hard as it was. It was at Albert's that I was exposed to more white people and began to see them for who they are and not putting all the blame for our troubles on all white people. I realized they knew nothing about the reality of our lives. I was still more comfortable with my own kin. Their world view was much more suitable for me.

Part 7
The Lubicon Struggle

Newcomers

The Muskotew Sakahikan Enowuk or Lubicon, as we were often referred to because we were mostly camped by Lubicon Lake, were a proud people. I am from the Lubicon band in northern Alberta. Our band never signed onto a treaty; therefore, my land was never protected from the newcomer's greed. We are still a proud people. My ancestors were the custodians of our land. When the newcomers took over it was very hard on everyone. For us to not be able to protect our ancestral lands from being ravaged by the greedy white faces was heartbreaking. The life we had lived was suddenly challenged by newcomers who decided that they wanted what we had.

Why oh why did things come to this? This was my people's land. We had a right to that land. The Creator had given it to us to protect. It had never happened in the history of our people.

When Treaty 8 came into being in 1899/1900, the Lubicon along with many others were missed by the treaty commissioners led by David Laird. The reason that the commissioners missed us, was because they stuck mainly to the Peace River and the Athabasca River. We, the Lubicon, lived inland and our land was not considered of much value anyway, so no one worried too much about my people. The efforts of some people from Lubicon Lake to sign on to Treaty 8 ended up backfiring. Some people traveled to Whitefish to ask for a reserve for the Lubicon, but the government agents simply signed them up with the Whitefish band. That has had severe consequences throughout the years and still has to this day. If you are signed up with a particular band, you have rights and privileges within that band only. The Lubicon were never the same band as the Whitefish. Our Lubicon people did not want to be, nor did the people of Whitefish feel the Lubicon should have rights within the Whitefish band. There was a housing allotment for every reserve, but there was never enough housing so that became a little challenging. The Lubicon, although they had the rights to claim benefits, did not want to take houses from the Whitefish band. That would just not be fair.

Then in the early thirties a most frightening rumour hit the northern communities. The white people in the cities were starving and they would come and live in our forest and take over Indian lands. The Lubicon held council as they realized they had to do something to protect their land and their rights. Indian Affairs was invited to come and discuss the issues. That was the first time Indian Affairs came to our community. At that time my people were promised a reserve on the shores of Lubicon Lake. That was the last we, the members, heard until oil was discovered.

1939 was a very significant year for us. Grouard Residential School first opened, and the kidnapping of the young people began. There was so much sorrow amongst my people. Ceremonies were held for the protection of the children. The Europeans did not pay attention to our pleas. They just continued to take the children year after year. In our community, the children had always come first. All activity revolved around the happiness and safety of the children. No one ate before them. We always protected and defended our children. Now we were prevented from even seeing them or speaking to them most of the time. I think that was the most devastating of all. Every household was in mourning for the loss of the children and grandchildren.

In 1952, oil was discovered on our land, but still not too many changes came about until one day in 1971, without any consultation or consent from my people, the province built an all-weather road into Lubicon territory. The leaders of our community met with the provincial government, and we were told that we were only squatters on provincial land and did not have any land to negotiate with, as there was no land allocated to us by the federal government, the province went ahead and issued permits for multinational oil companies to exploit our land.

There was much to learn as the Lubicon had not faced the white man's system before, and we had to fight for our land in the 'white' way. It was a challenging process to learn the new system we were facing but learn we did. We hired a community development worker, Fred Lennarson, to help us out. A caveat was registered against the disputed land. The caveat stipulated that we were contesting title to the land. The request was that nothing could proceed until the courts settled the dispute. No luck. The Government under Peter Lougheed changed the law and made it retroactive to before the caveat was filed, so they were not allowed to register it. That left us without legal protection.

We continued to try to negotiate for our land and at one time Indian Affairs officials told us that they recognized us as a separate, distinct society and they again promised us a reserve on the shores of Lubicon Lake. I remember the old people warning everyone that despite the promises, they were facing a bleak future and cautioned us to keep the old ways as much as we could. The elders predicted that some would forget their ancestor's ways. I remember my mother talking to me about these predictions. The Lubicon are a powerful people. This has been proven time and time again throughout history, with our fight for our land and when we took on the church, big corporations, and government. We keep fighting for our rights and we keep going, led by our sense of humour. We love to kid around. Sometimes it seems like that is all we have.

I have to say that some did not remain strong as they chose to take to alcohol and drugs and could not seem to collect themselves to be who they were taught to be. That was heartbreaking for the rest of us, but we just kept plugging along.

All the while, conflict between the treaty and non-treaty people was brewing. Metis people moved with the Hudson Bay Co. Some became traders themselves. They petitioned for land from the Alberta Provincial Government in the Big Lakes County. Probably because their fathers were white, they did get three settlements within the land base the Cree were trying to acquire from the Federal government. This was hard for my people to swallow, as we got nothing. We were the rightful custodians of that land. It wasn't that we minded sharing the land so much as the way it came about. The Metis were given the land stolen from my people by the Canadian government. Gift Lake, East Prairie and Peavine became their settlements.

When our land was overrun, our forests depleted, and our people were not able to sustain ourselves any longer, we had to do something to support our families. We were forced to engage in something that was totally against our belief system. There is an island out in Lesser Slave Lake, which had been claimed by the Dogrib Tribe. We just left them alone for many years, but in our desperation, we decided to chase them out as we needed the island to feed our people. Besides there was no legal claim to that land. We lived in peace without need for paperwork. There was plenty for everyone. When the Dogrib people moved on, dogs were left stranded and so we trained them to pull our sleighs. This way we could sustain our families as we could travel further to get game. This was new to our culture. Now in the face of scarcity, we had to do something, and we did.

We began a campaign to let others know about the plight of our people. People began supporting us when they found out. My role became to gather as much information as I could. Me and my friends snuck around in the bush and took pictures of the oil and gas wells and the devastation of our forests. We would hand those over to our local band government.

In 1983 the World Council of Churches officially backed us and concluded that what was happening to our people had genocidal consequences. I saw exactly what was happening and I agreed with their findings. It felt good to have such a powerful team on our side. As our hunting and gathering life disappeared, welfare went from 10% to 95%, as that was our only and last option to feed our families. There became very few new faces. Over an 18-month period in 1985-1986, out of 21 pregnancies only two babies survived to see daylight. No wonder my people were getting sicker in every way as time went on.

When we decided to boycott the Winter Olympics in Calgary, people from all over the world paid attention to our plight. Museums worldwide refused to lend artifacts to the Game's Indian art exhibition sponsored by Shell Oil. The world was paying attention.

The United Nations heard about our plight and did a study. In 1987 they concluded that we could not achieve effective legal or political redress in Canada, and they instructed Canada to do no more damage to the Lubicon, pending a hearing of human rights violations. The feds ignored the ruling. By this time there was so much anguish and in-fighting in my community that I decided to leave. Membership became an issue, land rights became an issue, the little compensation that came to our community became an issue. Who had the right to be leaders became an issue. Everything just deteriorated into chaos. For more than 100 years we struggled for official recognition from Canada. The Lubicon never signed away their traditional territory and still no-one listened.

There were 15 oil wells surrounding the Little Buffalo community, but not one penny came to the Lubicon people. The land and the water were polluted. With the clearcutting their means to support their families vanished. Sickness and death became rampant. without being able to take care of our mother the earth, without anything.

In 1989, the Alberta government sold softwood timber rights on the majority of Lubicon lands to Daishowa, a Japanese paper manufacturer, who went ahead with logging in the fall of 1990. The chief responded by warning all companies with operations on Lubicon territory that unauthorized developments would be removed without further notice. One late November night Buchanan's logging camp was torched, ending the logging for that season.

When Daishowa planned to return in the fall of 1991, Lubicon supporters began an international boycott of Daishowa products. Across Canada, major Daishowa customers began finding other suppliers for their paper bags. The commencement of boycott activity was instrumental in convincing Daishowa to cancel logging plans for the winter of 1991. But Daishowa still refused to make a clear, unequivocal commitment not to cut or to buy wood cut on unceded Lubicon territory until a land rights settlement had been reached with both governments. The boycott continued to grow, and each year Daishowa cut back from logging due to the mounting public pressure. By this time, it was too late. The animals left; our forests were no more. Our land was raped, our means of supporting ourselves were gone. It became a place of heartache. The provincial government did purchase a bunch of trailers, but did not invest in infrastructure, leaving the people without running water to their homes. One standing joke was that we had running water. We could run to the pumphouse and get it. People moved away from the community. Still, many fought on. In 2013, the band voted in a new chief, my relation, Billy Joe Laboucan. With Billy Joe as chief we had renewed hope for a better future.

Amnesty International Report

In 1987 after three years of study a UN Human rights committee states the the Lubicon cannot achieve effective legal or political redress in Canada.

1990 Amnesty International reported "...the basic health and resistance to infection of community members has deteriorated dramatically. The lack of running water and sanitary facilities in the community, needed to replace the traditional systems of water and sanitary management... is leading to the development of diseases associated with poverty and poor sanitary and health conditions." Lubicon complaint upheld by the United Nations Human Rights Committee in 1990

Lubicon Lake Nation General Election 2013 held May 30, 2013 at 1:00pm

OIL AND GAS DEVELOPMENT ON LUBICON LAND

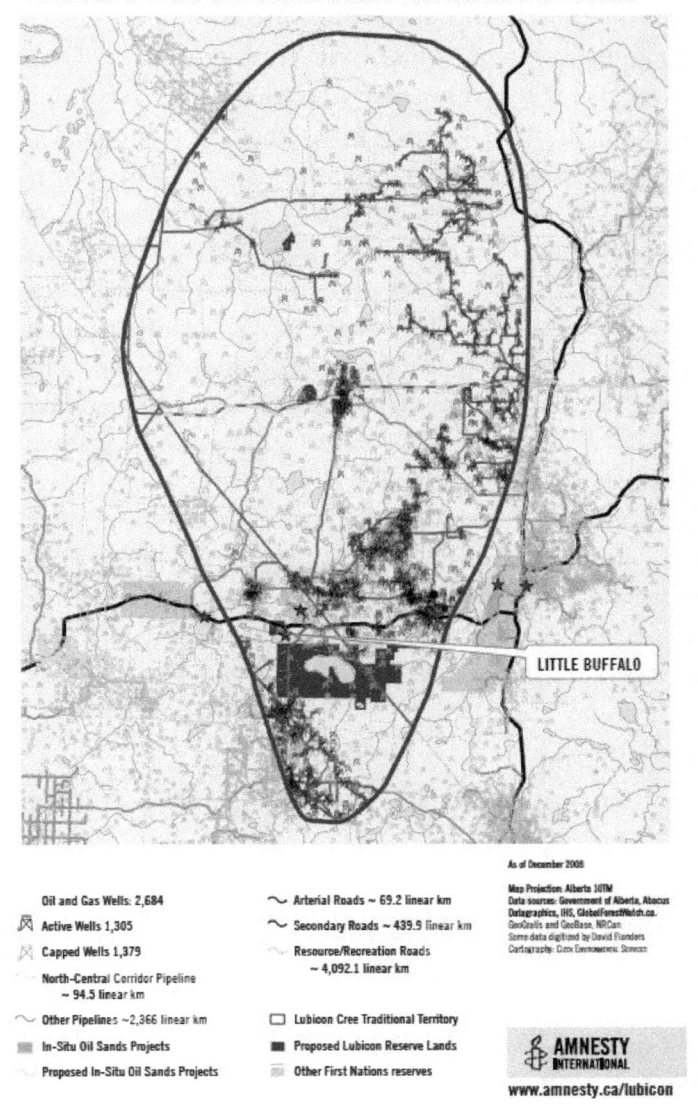

Oil and Gas Wells: 2,684
Active Wells 1,305
Capped Wells 1,379
North-Central Corridor Pipeline ~ 94.5 linear km
Other Pipelines ~2,366 linear km
In-Situ Oil Sands Projects
Proposed In-Situ Oil Sands Projects

Arterial Roads ~ 69.2 linear km
Secondary Roads ~ 439.9 linear km
Resource/Recreation Roads ~ 4,092.1 linear km
Lubicon Cree Traditional Territory
Proposed Lubicon Reserve Lands
Other First Nations reserves

As of December 2008
Map Projection: Alberta 10TM
Data sources: Government of Alberta, Abacus Datagraphics, IHS, GlobalForestWatch.ca, GeoGratis and GeoBase, NRCan
Some data digitized by David Flanders
Cartography: Cizek Environmental Services

AMNESTY INTERNATIONAL
www.amnesty.ca/lubicon

Over the last three decades, the province of Alberta has licensed more than 2600 oil and gas wells on the traditional territory of the Lubicon Cree. That's more than five wells for every Lubicon person. Territory that the Lubicon have relied on to hunt, fish and trap is now crisscrossed by more than 2400 km of oil and gas pipelines. In 2011, one of these pipelines spilled an estimated 28,000 barrels of crude oil into wetlands near the Lubicon community of Little Buffalo. It was one of the largest oil spills in Alberta history.

The Lubicon have never entered into a treaty with the Government of Canada. Nor have they ever given up any rights to their lands and territories. Once-promising efforts to negotiate an agreement to create a Lubicon reserve, and support the rebuilding of the Lubicon economy and society, have been stalled. Meanwhile, the federal and provincial governments have used their own failure to provide legal recognition of Lubicon lands as an excuse for excluding the Lubicon from decision-making over development in their lands and from a fair share in the revenue that has been generated. The Alberta government has acknowledging that it has brought in vast wealth from development of Lubicon land. In the midst of this wealth, the Lubicon live without running water. Today, more than 70% percent of Lubicon territory has been leased for future resource development, including oil sands extraction.

United Nations human rights bodies have repeatedly condemned the failure to protect Lubicon land from the impact of large-scale oil and gas development. The treatment of the Lubicon Cree stands as a powerful, emblematic example of the failure of governments in Canada to respect and uphold the legal rights of Indigenous peoples in the face of resource development.

Part 8
Reflections

True elder

I have given much thought about how to figure out the difference between a true elder and one who may claim to be but is not. These are some of the criteria I learned to recognize. The most common recognition of a true elder would be someone who has much knowledge from the experiences of life, or they can on rare occasion be a younger person who is gifted with special spiritual knowledge. All will live in reverence for all nature beings. A true elder will only leave behind their footprint as they travel on Mother Earth. They always express their gratitude for the gifts of food and the guidance received. They will know the protocol of the plants and animals and will always respect it. They may also know many warrior tales of morals and values.

The keepers of the wisdom are not generally called by their name but will be addressed as the grandmothers or grandfathers of the tribe. Even a very young, gifted person will be addressed as a grandfather or grandmother. They are recognized as such because they are close to God or Creator and will seek and receive guidance in that way. They know of the wisdom passed which is not from mankind, but guidance from above.

We have true pipe carriers of varying ages, so age on its own is not an indication of authenticity. A few children are seen by the wisdom keepers as having special spiritual knowledge far more profound than other children of the same age. They will be given special guidance of the ancient wisdom at a very young age. They will often spend more time with the elders than with their parents. It is recognized that these young people have evolved spiritually more quickly, and they are in great need of guidance from the ancients. Such a young elder will undergo the lessons of self-discovery, self-mastery and enlightenment. He or she would be in tune with the universe and the Creator. All true elders will understand both the seen and the unseen forces of manifestations of the Creator and the star people. Such elders could also be classified as prophets, as healers and teachers of good and positive ways. It is often difficult to find such elders as they or their family would not brag or advertise their sacred gifts. The communities know who they are and will take guidance from them. It is up to the seekers to find such elders and their name would only be revealed to true seekers.

One will never see an all-out conflict between the true elders. The path of the wisdom keepers forbids harming anyone, including ALL mankind. Each true elder commits to evolvement toward enlightenment and lives accordingly. They will meditate a lot and fast and do ceremonies that will bring them to the next level of knowing. Sometimes, if anyone abused those powers, they would lose them. Sacred pipes and other sacred items were known to mysteriously go back to the person who passed them the pipe in the first place.

Another gift some elders may have is the gift of the sweat lodge. As we share the different gifts, we must remember that each is very sacred and one not more so than another. The hot rocks used in a lodge are also called grandfathers. They carry that name because they are the oldest people on this earth. True elders do not put up a sweat lodge just because he or she wants to. It must be passed by an elder who has the right to perform this ritual. Rarely it can be passed from spirit, and if it is, one must go to an elder and offer tobacco gifts for him or her to interpret the vision. Then the seeker can begin their journey toward doing their own sweat lodge. Chances are that if they have been given that vision it will not take long before they learn what they need to know to be on their own.

In the lodge the four directions are of extreme importance as different teachings come from different directions. The teachings are all connected to the different life roles as they remind us of the path we travel. It is a big responsibility to carry the right to do the lodge, therefore not everyone has the consciousness to carry it. Because of the healing powers of the lodge, one must be strong in spirit and walk the good red road at all times.

Some elders have the gift to be able to guide others in a vision quest. It could have been passed to them through teachers who have had that experience for many years. Theses teachers assist those who wish to fast either for a vision or wisdom-seeking or enlightenment. When I began to go to vision quests, they would interpret for me the meaning of the visions which came to me. Only those who are gifted to do so, can. They will know the positive and negative energy areas that emanate from the earth, or between the earth and skies, the stars, and the cosmos. That is how they determine where to hold the vision quests. Such a gifted person will walk in the principles of prayerfulness and meditation for balance in body, mind, heart, and spirit that is necessary in order to guide and protect people in their quest for new knowledge. They know how to recognize and interpret the messages received.

Some elders take the natural path of herbal medicine. They are as respected as a doctor in the western society. They know and understand herbs, roots, plants, leaves and bark of trees and which berries are good for which ailment. They will also carry the knowledge of which animal parts are good for which illness. There is protocol of how to harvest these helpers as well as the specific combinations to use to cure an illness. You will never hear an authentic elder say that he or she is doing the healing. They will say that the God Creator is actually doing the work and they are only an agent or go-between for that work. If anyone claims that the work is anything but that, it should be a warning for you that this person is sadly misguided. He or she will pay the price for this blasphemy. Even Jesus said, "I can of my own self do nothing. It is my Father who worketh through me." Native people are very aware that this is actually the process.

This knowledge will be passed only to the person who has the right to carry it. They will have all the characteristics of a true elder. It is not my place to speak much on this subject, as I know far too little. I know only what I have seen and heard. I do want to caution everyone who seeks this kind of help to make sure they are dealing with someone who has been passed this knowledge in a legitimate way from those who know. Although I have been there when the herbs are prepared, it has not been passed to me to share it. I do not know many of the healing herbs or the protocol to gather them. I do have a few, but not many. This is another reason I will not call myself an elder. Those who have many medicines and know how to take them and what all can cure are the real elders. Please make sure when you see someone, they are referred by a reliable source and research from others you trust.

Popcorn elders

Some people will pass themselves off as elders when in actuality they have not received their knowledge from those who know or been passed this special knowledge spiritually. I call these people 'popcorn elders' because I say they got their license out of a popcorn box. I made errors in my search for the keepers of the true wisdom of the ancients, but it taught me well to recognize the difference between the genuine and the popcorn elders.

I learned over time that these people can only take you a very short distance in your evolvement.

As one elder said, you can have one handful or one truckload of sweetgrass and do the ceremonies, but if one does not improve purity of attitude and behaviour of daily balanced living, all the ceremonies will prove to be of no avail. If the ceremonies do not bring inner peace and teachings of harmony to the seekers, they are superficial and useless. The popcorn elders will bring you down. It is very hard to first unlearn the egoism which the popcorn elders teach. That unlearning is a prerequisite before anyone could continue on the path of true actualization. The true elder will help with this process, but it may be very painful for the seeker as finding out, that what one thought to be true is not. That teaching was most difficult, and I had to fast and meditate in order to understand where I went wrong. Learning my own true potential was hard work. There is no shortcut. If one is willing and actually does the work, they will be rewarded with a greater understanding and the ability to one day help others on their path.

Seekers who have sat with a popcorn elder, have most often come away confused, upset, and frustrated, because their expectations were not met. Many have been misled by the misused term "elder" and therefore did not find the answers to their quest. Some have been misdirected to seek out conjurers, sorcerers or others who tamper in the evil. They are the lost ones. These people have hurt the true seekers and true traditional wisdom keepers. This has led many both Native and Non-Native to believe that all our ways are bad, and sadly that our medicine is all bad. This has made it difficult at times to admit publicly that you are involved in Native prayerful rituals and ways of thanksgiving and gratefulness for all of nature's gifts. This has resulted in many gifted young people to simply give up, so they do not seek out the wisdom of the ancients (Kee-tee-aye-ak). Bullshit is bullshit and when you step in it, you know very well it's bullshit.

Those who go ahead and make a pipe or purchase one are taking a shortcut that is in no way earned. It is sad that people are doing that. Their pipe may actually be useless in that the holder will not be passed the knowledge and wisdom that would be passed to one that has done the sacrifice to earn it. It is difficult for the beginners who decide to follow the traditional way to know the difference. There are signs and signals one can look for. Lifestyle is one thing to look at. Their words are another. If they display signs of anger, then they have not done the work required. If you are very quiet and pray from the heart, you will most likely get the guidance you need. Your answers are available on a spiritual level through meditation and fasting. If you are bothered in your heart, follow that, and find someone who may be better for you. A person who has earned the right to carry a pipe will be kind, humble, honest and have empathy. You can feel his/her spiritual connection. He/she will walk in the understanding of the greater purpose of life. Through quiet meditation and participating in sweat lodges, you will get your answers as to if the chosen elder is good for you to learn from.

When you meet someone, you feel may not be trustworthy, and you are concerned about getting hurt, your best protection is to believe with all your mind, heart and spirit that you are a child of the Creator who will surround you with pure white light of love and power of protection. Then no harm will come to you. There is nothing to fear but fear itself when you walk in that light.

Another misuse of the term 'elder' occurs when some people refer to grandmothers and grandfathers who have walked this earth for many cycles, but who may not have taken the path of the ancients. They may not know or even believe in Native traditional ways. They may not know about the sacred pipe, the bundles or the protocol of taking care of these things and others. He/she may not know Mother Earth's sacred herbs, or the teachings of the moon seasons. They may not know the natural order of all life, or the universal intelligence, which is the guide to balance of all creation. I call these people simply 'old people,' but we do respect them, as they have a lot of living experience and have good information to share.

Churchianity vs Christianity

Now in my autumn years I have a lot of time for reflection. I often compare the elders' teachings with those things that happened to us at the hands of the churches and how different it was from the teachings of Christianity.

I believe God was used as an excuse. I do not believe evil is based in true Christianity. It is 'churchianity.' For me there is a distinct difference. I think some of the priests and nuns lost their way and used the church and their false God to do the horrible things they did. I do not believe it was the will of a true God to hurt even one child. It was only the will of the church. I believe it was the belief of the churches that kidnapped our children. It was not a Christian thing to do. In this context I use the term 'Indian' as that was what we were referred to in those days. Most Indian agents, priests and nuns had such a low view of us and that was hard to deal with. When our six-year-old children were constantly told how useless and evil they and their parents and grandparents were, it left its mark.

The newcomers used their power over us to withhold food or have us arrested at every turn. If the people on the reservations snuck away to visit their relatives and were caught, they were likely arrested and kept in jail for thirty days. Our people who lived on the reservations were not allowed to do our sacred ceremonies as they were heathen in the eyes of the 'white.' Our people on the reserves were forbidden to dance. The churches certainly created a problem for us when they labelled these things as pagan. Any practice outside their 'churchianity' was unfounded in reality and of the devil. I would watch the old ones quietly smile, as they knew that these church people with their aggressive attitude did not know much. The elders knew that they were not ready to listen and learn.

It was so sad as the churches continued their physical, mental, emotional and spiritual abuse without any respect for our Mother, the Earth. We talked about how for generations the empire builders around the world persecuted, prosecuted, discredited and herded traditional people into small pockets of poor land as they took over absolute control. Most people who decide to live a simple natural life have been overrun by the aggressive humans, without respect for all creatures of the great mystery, universe or Creator.

We did not believe that a just and true God would allow such atrocities, so much evil. It had to be a manifestation of the church people. It was clear that they were hiding behind the 'Christian' shields and did exactly as they pleased. They thought they were so superior to us. No one in Canada who had the power to make changes would listen to us, not government, not police, nobody. The church and the government tried to kill off our 50,000- year-old teachings. They told us we were nothing but heathens. When they taught our children that we were good for nothing, too many started to fall. We just lost it. Men began yelling at women, women began yelling at children. We just lost it! Thinking about it now clarifies why so many of us became so broken. The newcomers did everything in their power to destroy our spirits when they tried to destroy the traditional ways of our ancestors. Our spirituality was central to our very being. They did not fully succeed. We're still here!

John O'Sullivan, a journalist, articulated in 1845, that it was a God given right that North America was to become a capitalistic democracy with a transformation of landscape, culture and religious beliefs. He called it the manifest destiny. It became a justification for the churches and governments to take over. They used large manifest destiny posters to frighten us all into believing that there was only one way to salvation. Our way was a destiny straight to hell. It was all very confusing, as our ancestors did not believe in heaven or hell. They knew that if you did something to hurt other people or nature, you would pay. We believed in karma, but that in the end we would all be in the spirit world. The elders did not believe Jesus ever meant for us to suffer as we did with the separations, the sexual abuse and the corporal punishment the church inflicted on us. That is 'churchianity,' not Christianity. We believed that Jesus was a special messenger sent to this earth to teach kindness and caring for all people.

To assure that the 'Christian' belief system was adhered to, the government placed a resident Indian agent, who would readily report to the authorities every time anyone didn't follow the rules set out by them. Although the Lubicon didn't have a resident Indian agent, we were still hounded by the priests and the police when they paid us a visit, but no one was there on a daily basis.

They did however take our children, including myself. Many never returned to our community. Many took to the bottle, many just got lost. The crazy part was that we were told that the Christians came to help, that they would teach us how to have a better life, how to behave like them, how to think like them, how to pray like them and how to be like them. If we followed their way, we would have everlasting life. If we did not convert, our path was straight to hell.

The church teachings broke the code of having no more than four children per family. One for each direction. Four is a special balancing number as in earth, water, wind/air and fire or spring, summer, fall, and winter and east, north, west, and south, just to name a few. There was an odd exception to this as the seventh child of the seventh child is said to possess special healing powers, so with guidance a family may decide to carry on this tradition. When the Catholics told us that family planning was evil, the young who had converted began to have big families; they did not understand the consequences of overpopulation.

The old ones talked about the fact that the priests no longer had spiritual powers because they killed Jesus. The true elders know that there will be consequences if they abuse their gifts. They have seen how priests are not happy when they have broken the spiritual laws of their God. We did not want to be unhappy like that priest that broke our pipe.

Many times, through the years, Christians would try to convert me to their way of thinking as Christians do. Mostly I would not say much in their presence. They were constant reminders of my painful memories of my time in residential school and it was just too painful for me to get into a discussion with them. I try to respect other teachings as I want others to respect mine. When someone became too insulting telling me that they knew what was best for me, I could not be quiet any longer. I would have to give them a teaching. I would tell them that their way is all about 'Churchianity.' There is a big difference between 'Churchianity' and Christianity. Christianity is all about love, caring, sharing and tolerance. It is not too different from what I was taught from my people. True Christians, as true elders will recognize and have respect for all the holy teachers who walk this earth. Churchianity is all about power and control. I do not want to have anything to do with those who try to control others. They have no respect for our souls. We are a free people who follow the way of the Creator's teachings of caring and respecting all creation. I respect you even if I don't agree with you, but your way of disrespect for my people is not for me.

We have such a need for free thinkers and free spirits. Only when you are not boxed in by doctrine can we reach our full potential. Everyone is given a way to do things. I have mine and I expect others to honour that, as I would not interfere with their way. I just know that my elders taught that we had to have respect for other's beliefs, but at the same time others needed to have respect for ours. Churchianity does not always reflect those teachings. It is just not for me. In the long-term, positive will win over negative. It allows one to stand strong in their own power and gives strength to leave the bad behind.

Sadly, some people including the pedophile preachers do not understand this simple truth and the proper way to conduct one's life. Their attempt to force their own way on others shows that they have no regard for the fact that others may have different teachings, different ways which may also be a true way. I know that it is a challenge for those people, but forcing their way as opposed to sharing would be much less stressful and more peaceful.

In 2009 I did a presentation in Denmark. There were about fifty people in a circle and well into the presentation I shared about the abuse I suffered in residential school. I turned to one older gentleman in the group and said "If you really love a child, you cannot abuse them in that way. Right?" The gentleman said with great determination, "I do not agree." I was taken aback by his reply and repeated the question one more time, thinking that perhaps he had not understood my comment. One more time I got the same reply.

When we took a break, the gentleman disappeared. On the way out he said to my friend Jan, who had organized the presentation, "I am a Christian and I do not belong here."

When we returned to the circle, I noticed the man had left, but I carried on with the teachings. Still it bothered me that I never had a chance to make peace with him, as I felt things were left in a not good way and I wanted to talk to him further. At the end of the session Jan told me that he was the local priest, and I asked Jan if he thought he could find him. I do not like it when people go away angry. For the rest of the week Jan tried to make a connection with no luck.

To this day it bothers me that I had to leave the country without making peace with the priest. It is not our way to leave things unsettled.

White Buffalo

I think the most sacred story of my life began one year: I think it was 2011 when my friend Randal Kabatoff was driving along highway 11 just east of Sylvan Lake, and he spotted four white buffalo. He was overwhelmed by the sight as he knew how sacred the white buffalo was to his Native friends. He immediately contacted me to tell me about this most sacred thing he had seen. I got goose bumps all over and knew that something had to be done. This was such a rare occasion as there is only 1 in 10 million births of a white buffalo and he saw four together.

The legend of the white buffalo stems far back in our history. A long time ago the Lakota people were short of food and they sent two young scouts to look for meat. They came across a most beautiful young woman dressed in a white dress, with long black hair and dark eyes. One young man went lusting after her as she was so beautiful, while the other held back. When he got very close to her, a white cloud encompassed them both. Soon the cloud disappeared and only the white- clad woman stood and at her feet was a pile of bones belonging to the man who lusted for her.

The other became so afraid, but she told him that she would not harm him because she could see into his heart and he was not the same as the other man. She told him to go back to his people and tell them to prepare a feast for the next day and she would come and give them gifts. He did as he was told and the next day she appeared to the people. She brought the sacred pipe and taught them how to use it for prayer. She brought the seven laws by which we must live, the laws of respect, love, honesty, humbleness, courage, wisdom and truth. She taught seven ceremonies and seven songs. When she turned to leave, she rolled over on the ground four times, each time changing color for each race of the world. The last was the white color and then she suddenly turned into a white buffalo calf as she ran away.

On August 20th, 1994, a white buffalo calf named Miracle was born at the Heider Ranch in Wisconsin. Thousands came as she was considered to be a sacred symbol of renewal of humanity between all peoples and races around the world, and a reminder of the first teachings of the White Buffalo Calf Woman.

Randal and I contacted the owners of the white buffalo and asked if we could do some ceremonies at the farm. It was such a special event and it needed to be honored in ceremony. They gave us permission and we prepared for a series of four ceremonies, one each year for four years. We invited many people, and I gave tobacco to some elders to come, but they were not able to make it, so Randal, who is a white man, became my helper. I guess that was the way it was supposed to be. Native women from Saskatchewan, my whiz kid niece, and some other close friends, did the sacred cooking for the feasts. Ruby, the owner, invited friends who all respected deeply what was happening.

He told us the story of the bull that sired most of the calves. Ruby was travelling in the States, and he won a big jackpot at a casino. He felt this money had come to him for a special purpose. The next day he found out about a white buffalo that was for sale and he knew immediately what the money was for. He purchased it and named him Jackpot. Coincidently he was the great grandson of Miracle. He committed right then and there that no white buffalo would be butchered for meat. They will be able to live a full, long life on his ranch.

The third year the owner released the white buffalo into the pasture where we had the ceremony. Some wandered close and joined us. All were ever so docile and seemed to enjoy what was happening. When I was talking to the people, I suddenly felt a nudge on my shoulder. When I turned my head, it was a small white calf that rubbed its nose up against me. I was completely overwhelmed by that sacred experience. We did three ceremonies at the ranch, but the family decided that it was too much to have any more, so we moved the last one to Silver Sands, near Onoway, Alberta. It was a blessed time for all.

I am fortunate to be able to still do ceremonies with support from friends. We did some at Bob Holm's buffalo ranch, where I passed on the honour of being watchers to four people. A watcher's responsibility is to watch and take action when any of the Creators creations are being hurt. It is a big responsibility and not to be taken lightly.

Another Ceremony that we did was the frog ceremony. It is performed near water as the frogs live both on land and in the water. I am still called out to do pipe ceremonies and prayers for different organizations and that makes me very happy.

For as long as I am able, I will celebrate the four seasons in ceremony. Spring, mid-summer, fall and winter. These are so important to keep harmony with the changes of our seasons.

I am enjoying what time I have left on my earth journey. I think it will not be long before I move on.

Prophesies

I often think about the prophesies of the old ones and see how much has come true already and how much is still to come. The elders had predictions of the future. One was that the European people would take over and destroy our way of life. Life as we know it would cease to exist. Hell was coming for our people and for Mother Earth. Over hundreds of years, the Ancients shared the prophesies.

I remember when I was a boy hearing the elders say, "For many generations we have heard that Mother Earth would suffer greatly with the coming of the pale faces. It will be the beginning of the end of time as we know it."

There will come from across the great salt water, a hairy-faced pale one. They will be dressed in strange clothing and wear head adornments. They will look and behave fiercely. They will arrive in a strange huge canoe that holds hundreds of them. They have strange beasts on the strange canoe. As the years pass other strange canoes will come to our shores. No women are heard or seen to come. As the years pass others will come and sweep over our people like a great wave. As they sweep over our people their very blood shall fall unto the blood of your people.

Predictions were that Mother Earth would be sliced up into squares by these newcomers and they would claim ownership of our Mother the Earth. Long strings would not allow the Native family travelers to walk on our Mother. That was confusing to many people as ownership was not a part of our belief system. Other predictions were that the newcomers would use a long thread that would allow people to speak together over long distances. Strange objects with people inside would fly in the sky. There would be a long black road for man and horses to walk on. The paved roads? These are but a few of the prophecies of our people. Many more have come to pass.

I have shared what I know and what I was taught. This is my teachings only and I know others differ slightly. I do not profess to have all the answers in fact I have more questions than answers.

A prediction the elders made years prior to European contact was that when the blood of Mother Earth would be sold, it would bring much spiritual and physical sickness. It would be a warning sign that the end was near. It was said that our people had gone into a deep sleep, but when the eagle lands on the moon we will start to wake up. When Armstrong landed on the moon, his first words were, "The Eagle has landed," and that is when our people started to rally.

I heard the elders speak about the four stages that our Earth has passed through, the first being the age of fire, then the age of ice, the age of water and now we are in the fourth stage, the age of the wind. The native people have lived through those stages here on Turtle Island. If the people do not follow our cosmic guides, the wind will cleanse this earth. Will mankind survive?

One prediction that was often spoken about was that the grandfathers (north and south pole) will exchange places. When that happens Mother Earth will once again be cleansed. One of many predictions for earth's future.

There was a prophecy from the ancients that was passed from generation to generation; The loss of women's virtues would mark the decline of the Native people. This prophesy has come to pass with the coming of those from overseas who brought the social change to sexual freedom. When the young girls returned from residential school, they began the practice of having unwanted, undeserved babies, who did not grow harmoniously in the mother's womb, who did not grow up with the seven sacred teachings. Too many grew up with alcohol and lost the knowledge of their sacredness as bearers of the new faces yet to come. They did not understand that sexuality is very sacred and should not be fooled with. All in all, it has been a total disaster. The other part of this prophesy was that the Native women will once again regain purity and virtue, which will mark the rise of the Native people once again to their former humble and proud selves.

And the graveyards continue to look like newly plowed fields.

Struggles

I think a lot these days about my journey and the journey of my people.

My challenges with life and my attempt to gain respect for myself and my people has taken my whole lifetime and those who came before me and will continue with the coming faces. In 1867, the newcomers to our land decided to create a country for themselves, which became the Dominion of Canada under the British Empire. The English monarchy drew up treaties with us. In reality, the treaties enabled the Dominion of Canada to take all the land they wanted for the newcomers. There was no consultation with my people. We were told that we would receive rations and a yearly payment of five dollars. Every year on treaty days, at which time we still gather, the RCMP come in their red serge and hand every band member their five-dollar bill. That has been a ritual since the late 1800's and we have not had a raise since. The government officials who approached us, made us believe that it was an agreement of mutual benefit; not so in actuality, the treaties gave the newcomers full control, not only of our land, but also over almost all aspects of Native society.

After the Dominion of Canada took our land they proceeded to break their own agreements. They took more land than was originally 'agreed' upon, resulting in many of the modern-day land claims, which are now before the courts. We have struggled to keep the spirit of the treaties between us and the English crown in place as we saw them. Every treaty signed in Canada differs a little according to the terms 'agreed' upon. The Indian Act, passed in 1876, was the Canadian government's way of enforcing their interpretation of what they decided the purpose of the treaties were, again with no consultation with the First Nations.

The Indian agents who were appointed by the government were given full control of reservations. If their directions were not followed, we risked going to jail or they could hold back the rations that we were promised, resulting in hunger. Our movements were restricted, and we could no longer hunt and fish wherever we needed to in order to sustain our families.

In 1894 it became mandatory for all native children to go to residential school. In 1925 the act was amended banning all aspects of traditional ceremonies, and dancing. That left us without being able to practice our spiritual ceremonies, or to pray the way we were taught from the Creator, or to even raise our own children. The Dominion of Canada also forbade my people from hiring a lawyer, nor did they allow us to trade off the reserve. Looking back, I think the purpose was to make things so bad that the Indian would incorporate into the Euro-Canadian population. We entered a very dark time in our history. The pain of it all was overwhelming.

We are not a dominant people. We believe in equality for all, but we had no say. We were left powerless. The intent to take the Indian out of us so we would want to become 'white,' failed miserably. As a result, we are now dealing with intergenerational trauma. We were even restricted from gathering for any purpose, so it put an end to the practice of governance by all the people in our communities. The Indian Act replaced our traditional ways of governing ourselves, with the present-day band chief and council system. The rights of everyone else in the community having a say was no more. Only those of 'good' character could run for office. The Indian agents decided who was of good character. When a few brave and very intelligent tribal members did, against all odds, get a university degree, the government took their Indian status away. Now they were supposed to be 'white.' Anyone joining the armed forces were made to deny their status. For some of the young braves who did fight in the wars, it was a way to escape life on the reserve and see the world. Others understood that their white brothers and sisters needed their support to protect Canada. When our warrioes returned from overseas, they were denied membership in the Legion, the most highly respected organization for veterans in Canada.

Tough decisions had to be made in those early days. We were expected to deny our heritage. If we crossed over to the 'white' ways our people often called us apples. We were caught between a rock and a hard place with so many challenges no matter which way we turned.

Restricting us from going to a bar or having a drink was just another reminder that the dominant society made all the decisions about what they thought was good for us. It never stopped those who made the choice to partake in alcohol to do so. The seers saw the future and it was not good.

The traditional elders insisted that the nomadic life they were accustomed to far surpassed in goodness and wellbeing the new lifestyle imposed on the reserves.

If you tie a horse to a peg in the ground and give him enough rope to wander within a restricted space, even if there is enough food, his spirit will be broken. Also, he will only know that area he is restricted to. If he is not moved, he will live and die knowing and digesting only that little circle. That has been our battle.

If the Indian agent did not agree to let us leave the reserve, to collect medicines or hunt, and we went anyway, the consequences was most often jail. As we had no knowledge or history of their cruel ways, we got trapped into the situation. We had feared nobody before the Indian agent came along. Now we had to fear being put in cages like animals.

Our reserves mostly had poor lands and no real opportunity for economic development opportunities. Some people were provided with farming equipment, but we were not farmers and besides we were mostly allotted the poorest land. The plan was doomed to fail and fail it did.

When we were locked up in the white man's cages, all the joy and happiness were gone, but still we would gather and tell funny stories to help lift our spirits, even for a little while. When we were forbidden to gather, we always found a way.

We were put to shame for the poverty and poor education, even though it was the 'whites' who caused it. Our graveyards have been like a newly plowed field with many fresh graves due to premature deaths. My people died from diseases brought in from Europe, they died from suicides, they died from alcohol abuse, from murder, especially of our women who left the reserves.

Even with this history, our community consider the treaties as a sacred agreement, which was to last as long as the grass grows and the rivers flow.

It is the Indian Act we mostly struggle with because that is the oppressive legislation passed in by the Canadian government. It was only in a 1951 amendment to the Indian Act that some restrictions were lifted. After that we were permitted to reclaim our traditional ceremonies and community events.

Once again, we could pray and dance. After that amendment we could seek legal advice and fight for our rights in the white man's courts.

Still, the women who married a non-Native person were stripped of their treaty status. That was just another way for the government to get rid of their responsibilities. Our society had always been a matriarchal society; the government changed all that and made the lineage based on the male members of the community. Laws were made that took away a woman's rights if she was widowed or separated. We fought hard for the women to regain their recognition – which finally came about in 1985. After a long and hard-fought battle, Bill C-31 was passed reinstating our women. Some of their future generations will lose their status. When that happens there will be more confrontations with the government. It is not the treaties per se we fight against. It is broken treaties; it is the Indian Act. It is the terrible law which put all the power into the hands of the Canadian government.

I will never forget our battle in 1969. The Canadian government under Prime Minister Pierre Elliot Trudeau introduced a white paper, scrapping the Indian Act all together. The government saw this as a good thing, as the Native people would then become like the white, without recognition that they were a distinct society. It would wipe out the reservations and give land ownership to individuals.

At that time the Indian Association of Alberta was a strong lobbying group for my people. Harold Cardinal led a whole team of people, of which I was one, to put a stop to that and went to Ottawa to present the Red Paper. It was developed by my people and was intended to stop the one-sided decisions out of Ottawa.

We all saw that if the White Paper was to be incorporated, it would be the end of our fight for sovereignty and self governance over the little bit of land that we were able to hang onto. It was definitely a plan to divide and conquer. We would no longer have special status as a people.

As Harold Cardinal explained: "We do not want the Indian Act retained because it is a good piece of legislation. It isn't. It is discriminatory from start to finish. But it is a lever in our hands and an embarrassment to the government, as it should be. No just society and no society with even pretentions to being just can long tolerate such a piece of legislation, but we would rather continue to live in bondage under the inequitable Indian Act, than surrender our sacred rights. Any time the government wants to honour its obligations to us, we are more than happy to help devise new Indian legislation. In the end the government backed down. That was a turning point for our people. We took our power and we won. Thank you, Creator, the government of Canada was not able to annihilate our traditional ways no matter how hard they tried. Despite the prohibitions of the Indian Act, we remained who we are. We still do what we need to do.

We are a distinct society with an international recognition of such through the treaty agreements. We want to remain a distinct society. We were here first; we have lived here for thousands of years. We believe that the Creator gave us this land to live on and take care of. All peoples were given land somewhere for that purpose.

Hear me See me Feel me

This is my story. This is our story.

We have always had to struggle for everything in order to survive as a people, but through thick and thin we have survived. Now I see many getting their education and those who remember the traditional teachings are becoming a force to be reckoned with. We have long hair because it is our antenna. Long hair is our antenna to Mother Earth, to water and to air. So, if you have no hair, you play with fire. You are going to destroy Mother Earth and that is what the white people have done ever since they arrived. They should not be taking that gas and oil; it belongs where it is. Everything that befalls Mother Earth will befall us. So my antenna keeps me straight, and I will live by it. No one should be sending satellite dishes out there, that is what I heard from the elders. When people go up to the moon and to Mars, they send fire.

I am afraid that if we do not stop placing most of our attention on material things and only fundamental and superficial importance on our true spiritual selves, we will squander life away with the materialistic mentality. If we do not have some understanding of God, Creator, universal intelligence, and nature connection, we will not have the awareness and consciousness of the natural order of all life and Mother Earth. It will be a difficult walk for us today.

There are two sides to everything, but most newcomers hear only the negative side of the indigenous people, as if we are a problem for them. That is why most non-native people just do not want to learn from us. All these years they were taught how we are inferior and did not even have a written language. Well, we did, but according to the Euro/Canadians history we did not. All native people had a written language, and we see these syllabics in many places today, especially on official band buildings. All differ according to the language groups. We have had a written language since time immemorial. James Evans is credited with bringing the Cree syllabics to the people. Why would he not teach the English writing instead? Today you will see the local syllabics along with the English on many road signs including between Vancouver and Whistler in British Columbia. Almost all road signs on reserves are now written in their traditional language with traditional syllabics, along with the English. Following is an example of the Cree syllabics.

▽	é	△	i	▷	o-u	◁	a	•o	w
⊓	mé	Γ	mi	⌐	mo-u	L	ma	c	m
U	té	∩	ti	⊃	to	C	ta	,	t
ꟼ	ké	ᑭ	ki	ᑯ	ko-u	ᑲ	ka	ˋ	k
⊓	né	ᑌ	ni	ᑎ	no-u	ᑎ	na	ᕽ	n
⊓	lé	ᒥ	li	ᒧ	lo-u	ᒪ	la	s	l
ᒉ	ré	ᒋ	ri	ᒍ	ro-u	ᒐ	ra	z	r
ᒉ	sé	ᓯ	si	ᓱ	so-u	ᓴ	sa	n	s
ᐸ	yé	ᐳ	yi	ᐰ	yo-u	ᐯ	ya	+	y
∩	tché	∩	tchi	∪	tcho	∪	tcha	-	tch
V	pé	∧	pi	>	po	<	pa	ı	p
▽•	we	△•	wi	▷•	wo	◁•	wa		
▽•o	wew	△•o	wiw	▷•o	wow	◁•o	waw		

Cree Syllabics. Also taught in our education program.

 The empire builders, are scientifically explaining away his God Creator with a theory that a large cosmic explosion of sorts caused a cosmic creative reaction. The debates continue and they do become heated at times as everyone has a different notion of Creator and Creation. However, heated the debates become, almost everyone agrees there is a 'force' of some kind to cause life to be as we know it. Creation or evolution makes no difference as I see it. The fact remains that a 'force,' a God, if you will, a Great Spirit caused the creation of our Mother Earth and all life forms. Maybe the Great Spirit or God created the explosion. To our Native people this knowledge is not worth the verbal blasts, the heated arguments and wars that exist today. It is as it is. It is taken in our teachings that the Great Spirit is everywhere and is still causing changes or creating if you will. This is denied by those that do as they please and manhandles the things that are.

The empire builders have been hard-headed and hard-hearted to the point that for many, their God has become meaningless quotes of scriptures. They have introduced science, huge mansions, fancy cars and money, money, money. If the empire builders can explain away their God Creator, then we as a people do not mean much either. Perhaps we are simply in the way of progress as they define it. Technology has become the master and in the process of mastery is garbaging life out of existence through pollution creation. The sad thing is that mankind is being swept right along with it. I feel that if people don't listen it will soon be too late. To what lengths will the progress be allowed to happen? I don't know.

If humanity does not change and take better care of our Mother, the Earth, I am afraid for all people. When we only take what we need for our own survival, there is enough for everyone. Things can improve if the people listen to the 'earth keepers.' First of all, look upon us as people with morals, ethics and values. We are people with a mind, heart and spirit, contrary to the way we have been portrayed by governments, historians, media, the movie industry and missionaries, who have been a big influence on the way non-Native Canadians see us. Everyone who believed these sources had very little direct contact with our people. Without direct contact, how could the newcomers know better? When people hear only negative, they believe it. The missionaries labelled us as primitive, savages and pagans and the newcomers believed it. Many of those labels are still with us today. In those early days, the newcomers had so much faith in the churches, so what else could they believe? How could the people go against the institutions who had brainwashed them into believing their teachings? Many early documents proving this are available in archives all across the country if anyone desires to read them for themselves.

Those that came under the pretense to help and 'save' us, resulted in just the opposite happening. It clearly showed that they hid behind the Christian shields and the deceit is evident even to this day. This knowledge and observation have taught Native people never to stray from their teachings. The traditional people do not retaliate as they know they are as bad as the perpetrator, and they do not want to go there. We believe that God is here for all people.

We must walk in a good way in the teachings of our Creator. We must strive to walk in that inner peace and harmony. The beings who have not evolved to that level often remain in the past hurts and that in turn manifests itself in anger, resentment and other negative feelings and thoughts.

This may be of conscious or subconscious sources or perhaps in our spiritual minds, but negative thoughts can affect us all dramatically. I have witnessed where many of my people have grown to be adults, but the wounded child is still inside. I try to talk to them as it is so painful to watch. If some people do not turn their lives around and follow the traditional ways of thinking, even if they own their own businesses, or are in the workforce, life will be less than optimal for them. People can still make money as long as money does not become their God.

Although the Christians tried to destroy our traditional beliefs they did not succeed fully. I guess some of us were too tough. So many of the Christian beliefs are the same as ours. At least it would be nice if we could stand on common ground.

I feel that the government saw us through tunnel vision. They only saw their side, their way. They never looked at us as people with our own dreams and visions of what was good for us. The government could not or would not consider our truths. Their efforts to destroy all that was sacred backfired miserably.

There were moments in time, however, when we outwitted them, when the people took their power. I remember how we had loose floorboards under the heaters where the sacred things that were outlawed were kept. Everyone would be very quiet when strangers would come to our homes. Only after they left would everyone begin speaking again. No one had anything to discuss with these evil people. They never looked under our heaters. They never found everything.

Our people have never had a holy war like the Crusades. To shed blood over which tribe held the truth was never on our radar. Sure, we had minor skirmishes, but never over the monopoly of the Great Spirit. The old ones tried to share with our white brothers that we too had a path of truth, righteous living, rules of discipline and enlightenment given to us. It is written in nature, the animals, the birds, the water the trees, in the seasons and blowing in the wind. We consider all in nature as our 'relations' and we respect and take care of all our 'relations.' All can teach us something. The grass teaches us resilience. We walk on it, mow it down, dance on it and still it returns to stand tall. It does survive. The trees teach us the patience of stillness. The power to stand tall, the power to stand alone in its glory. The wolf teaches us about family and community relations and that we all have an important role. If we do not follow the pack's laws, we will be banished. Wolf taught us that banishment was the ultimate consequence if we broke with harmony in our community, and we could not or would not return to peace. Everyone placed on the earth has a purpose to fulfill. Every animal, every bird, every fish, every plant and every human. If one disappears it will affect all of us. That is why we fight so hard for every one of Creator's creations. That is why we keep fighting. It is for all mankind, all our brothers and sisters everywhere on our Mother the Earth we all live.

We have the answers, but no-one hears us. For the sake of all mankind, please do so! Climate change has been with us in the past and will continue in the future. It is a natural happening. Life in the past was different than life today. Today is different than it will be in the future, but if we do not take care, we will hit a wall. Mother Earth has always survived, and she always will. Will mankind survive? That is another question. If we do not listen, we will pay the price. It is what it is.

It is sad that one confused race would think they are so superior to everyone else and have the right to enslave our black brothers and treat us as they did. The anger, pain, confusion, and frustration are the results of domination and superiority attitude and not being seen or heard. That mentality was never a part of our people who lived in respect for our Mother the Earth and Creator and all creation. Europeans brought a different world view to this land, to our land. People whose view was tied to materialistic gain. People who have an egotistical mind with the main purpose being for their own benefit without thought for others, for nature or for any of the consequences of their actions. The empire builders will gain in materialistic things and feel they are a success, and better than others, but there is a price to pay for that kind of thinking. That mindset cannot relate to mystical experiences coming from within and from outer connections. Their attention is focused on their projects only and they are not open to contemplation from a meditative practice, where they can learn so much. The empire builders do not take the time or effort to understand that the connection to head and heart is imperative to becoming all that they can be, and so they pollute. We have watched this with heavy hearts. The newcomers broke the rules of the Great Mystery and ended up in a hurtful place. The heart connection is often lost and that is a loss to all. It is very painful to watch. If someone carries out a negative action toward others, everyone in their vicinity will be affected, even the people who it is not directed at. Verbal attacks against our people have had a very devastating effect. Hearing others being attacked is even worse than being attacked ourselves. The spiritually connected person will problem solve by quiet communication. Harmony will most likely prevail, if respect for others is taken into consideration.

A forceful mind cannot see the benefit of the spirit that dwells in the hearts of mankind. It is in the intuitive and instinctual that one finds the light. The egoistic mind cannot see this when it is brainwashed with the modern development and technological advances that the western education focusses on. The egoistic emotion is consumed with far too much false pride and clings to the emotions of anger, hurt and bitterness when things do not go their way. The openness of learning new concepts that do not fit in this mindset is generally not even considered. These people are very difficult for us to deal with as they are just not willing to listen and explore our truth. To them our people are inferior, and our teachings have no value. The more materialistically advanced a society becomes, the more often the simple-living people are squeezed out. We see how much we are losing out. It is sad that they don't.

We have a truth that differs from the newcomers. We have listened to the ancients, who were given a way to live which was based in partnership and connectedness with Creator and all creation. We received our knowledge from the manifestations from the universal Great Spirit, and our helpers.

The newcomers destroyed our pipes, our rattles, our drums and our bundles, which were the most sacred of all. All in an effort to destroy us and who we are and make us into good little English and French citizens. All under the banner of Canada. It didn't work then and it's not working now. Too many of my people are being incarcerated today. Too many of my people commit suicide.

Too many of my people have lost their spirit. Too many of my people are living a sick life. I'm not sure we can turn it around. I am afraid it is too late, but we can't give up. Too few people left that know the way of the ancients. Too sad for me. All these things I remember were predicted by the old people. That is why I cannot call myself an elder. I do not have nearly the powers of my ancestors. I am only a helper to the old ways. Sometimes it is so hard when I am not heard, when I am not seen for the person, I am, when no-one feels the sorrow in my heart, when no-one seems to care. Most white people only see a drunk Indian.

Our people are deep thinkers. We look at the bigger picture. Still our wisdom keepers are not heard. We have the answers for a good life. We can have the things that the newcomers bring and still have respect for and connectedness with Nature. Everyone may have to just slow down a little. That does not fit well with the newcomers as they are always in a hurry to make more money as quickly as possible. Making money their god is what has enabled industry to walk away leaving our land and water polluted. The reaction is likely to be very confrontational and without due care and attention you may be sucked into that same pit and become that way too. The problem with that is that if you are not like them in your core, you will likely lose in the short term as the stubborn mindset is very powerful in a negative way. You cannot be what you are not. If you are not egoistic, you are not. If you can walk away and let them talk to the air you win. Staying out of that energy as much as possible can be challenging for sure. The person that can walk away in a good way is by far the most powerful, the freest spirit.

The danger for us, the Earth keepers, is that the newcomers will continue to manhandle us into silence as they overpopulate Turtle Island – as they overpopulated Europe. If we, the Earth Keepers are not heard, the danger for the Earth, for Turtle Island and for the world is that we the people of nature too, will be pulled into the destructive ways of making the almighty dollar the most important while Mother Earth suffers. If we are not vigilant, we too may become extinct.

True freedom can only be found when one understands the connectedness and how we as humans fit into the bigger picture. Freedom carries the responsibility of being neither an attacker nor a defender. It is a state where no one can control or rule over you and you cannot rule over others. It is a state that cannot be affected by the imbalance of others. Freedom is only found in pure awareness of consciousness of being. Freedom to live in the awareness of consciousness is a simple way of life. A oneness with the universe here on earth and the universe of the spirit world.

There is another power which is even stronger than the negative. The power of the heart, of the spirit. The power of love. Love sends out an energy which will be felt by all people when they are in its presence. Even plants and animals can feel that energy. Science is beginning to catch up with the old wisdom.

The people who end up in the jails are people who have lost their way, their true power from their heart and Creator. We do have people in the jails now who can help the inmates restore themselves to balance. The work that I did so many years ago to make that help available to the inmates makes me feel good, because it is good.

By sharing these truths, I hope and pray that those who are seekers become aware that there is evil out there and if one buys into it, someone may get hurt. On the other hand, there is so much good in the true, traditional nature way. The true elder knows and lives these things. They are the essence of that close to perfect spiritual being, who gently passes spiritual wisdom from heart to heart with the seekers. All true teachers of peace, no matter where they are in the world, no matter what religion they belong to, know this simple truth.

I have shared much of that truth in the previous pages, and I do not want to repeat myself again. What I have shared is only the tip of the iceberg. Yes, there is much to contemplate and sometimes I feel very depressed about all that I have seen. Sometimes I am also lifted by something good and hope returns. When I meet up with the wisdom keepers, they often tell some good jokes and that lifts my spirit. When the talk got very serious someone would balance it off with a good funny story. We still do that. Today we understand that humour and laughter was what pulled us through all the terrible things that entered into our lives and communities with the coming of the pale faces. But we did pull through! We are still here!

I feel good about being able to help as many people as I could. I have to admit that some I could not help, because they didn't want to hear my words. Because of my raging years I understand that, and then I pray for them and ask the Creator to help them find their way back to a good place.

I am grateful that I have been a part of the old ways and am one of the few who have lived from 'smoke signals to cell phones.' I do my best to acknowledge and enjoy both the old and the new. After all, there are blessings in both. I like my truck and my cellphone, but I am totally at peace when I am in the bush by myself. That is when I learn the most and find comfort in solitude.

In reality the whites told us Indians that we were to be like them, but the white society didn't want to have anything to do with us. The reserves became full of pain, so there was no peaceful place for us. Our lives went from being a free roaming, fearless, happy people to being hurt and bitter and confined.

Today we too have become cluttered by the new world order. The material things, the noise, the fast pace we live and all the things we need to take care of in this modern world, all make our minds cluttered. When I think of the old people and what they knew and were able to do, it makes me realize just how much we have lost. Today we do have a choice to leave the reserves or stay but leaving to go to a hostile world is not easy. Some brave souls do go to attain a higher education. Others get lost in the inner cities. Some are successful in professional capacities.

Today we still dance, we can have our sacred ceremonies, we have schools on the reserves, but there is still a long way to go before the healing will be complete. Our graveyards are still like plowed fields, as many do not reach old age. Of those who are getting the western education, it is the people who also keep their old knowledge of the beauty ways that do best. Many today do walk proud in both worlds, and they are becoming a force to be reckoned with.

We did not, and to this day do not want to be like the Euro-Canadians. We do accept some things like education and earning our own living, but we also incorporate our traditional ways such as round dances, sun dances, pow wows, sweat lodges and other ceremonies.

Even those who went to residential school were never taught enough to function as full members in the newcomers' society, so fighting the white man in his way was not possible, until we learned their system. Most of the residential school time was spent in religious studies and doing the chores that kept the schools going. Emphasis was not placed on preparing the Native children to become full members of the newcomers' society. They learned very well what was wrong with their people, their ancestors.

Autumn years

As I look back on my youth and childhood, I prefer to remember the good times– the hunting, the fishing, the dancing, the ceremonies, the visiting and the learning. They far outweigh the negatives. I feel like I have struggled all my life. The only true peace I have ever had was when I was a young boy in my community. That is, it was great until I was kidnapped and sent to the invader's world, which was not like my world.

A good thing did happen in 2006 when I got a settlement from the government for the abuse I had suffered in residential school. I was able to buy a Ram 1500 truck and a camping trailer. I love that truck and camper because now I can go hunting without worrying about breaking down in the bush and I have a place to sleep, as I still travel to the ceremonies. I also have a nice place to sleep when I go to Lac Ste Anne every year.

In November of 2016 I got very ill. My whiz kid nieces became extremely alarmed and took care that I received all the best help. I know they were afraid for my life. I knew I would get better. Some of the doctors and nurses treated me good, but not all. I did get better, but it was a slow process. Sometimes my friends or nieces would come and take me out, so I could get a break from hospital food. That brought great comfort as I really had a hard time with the food. Sometimes I wondered if I would survive the diet, never mind my illness.

I did continue to get stronger and stronger and eventually I started walking the half kilometer to Kingsway Mall almost every day. That helped my spirit a lot. My friends and family would take me to the trees, and we would walk on dirt. That really helped me get more strength.

There have been so many changes in just my lifetime. I see now that each experience in my life journey, good or bad, was a teaching, even the most challenging. I'm not sure how many more generations it will take before my people will walk in harmony with the connectedness we understand. There are still a few who walk the old ways. Hopefully they will lead our people in a good way. I am not too optimistic though. Too many of my people are too broken.

Now I live in a small room. I have no choice but to accept my circumstances. For now, I need to accept things as they are. I do have my dreams of going hunting once again. I am happy that I can still hold ceremonies with some help. I have lived long, I have struggled much, but I am blessed for the opportunity to have done some good work, on this my earth walk. This is my story of living in harmony with Mother Earth, Nature and Creator and my struggle as I was forced to live the Euro/Canadian way. It is my story of how the two had to amalgamate in one lifetime. My purpose in sharing this is to give a little guidance to the coming faces and to share the fact that one can turn their lives around, even when we hit bottom. My earth journey has not been an easy one, but I know there is light after darkness. We can move toward that light. I know I am close to my journey back to the spirit world. I have not been perfect, but I did my best.

Henry finished his earth walk on April 14, 2018. He transitioned to the spirit world quietly and peacefully.

Billy Joe Laboucan, chief of the Lubicon Nation, was able to settle the longstanding land claim on October 24, 2018. Unfortunately, Henry was not here to see it.

Epilogue

I am the land of the Muskotew Sakahikan Enowuk. I am the Mother

I am the land in down north on Turtle Island, northwest North America, given to the animals, the fish the birds the plants, and the Muskotew Sakahikan Enowuk people of the Lubicon Nation as it is known today. Everyone lived peacefully on my body together since 'time immemorial.' There was joy and gratefulness for the riches I and our Father Creator provided for all. There was food and shelter for the four legged, the two legged, the swimming, the flying and the creeping ones. There was place and space for all to live and flourish. As the people of my land roamed from village to village everyone was welcomed in the land of the Muskotew Sakahikan Enowuk. The people danced and celebrated and were grateful for their riches. They hunted and fished and the enowuk (people) were joyful for the abundance and were rich in their hearts. The animals too were rich in my land of plenty. I was satisfied that things were as they should be. I the land, I the Mother saw this existence through thousands of years. One day another human arrived. A Moniyaw, a white man newcomer, That was the beginning of a new kind of life for my people.

Men who dressed in black robes like women came to my land, did not understand the natural laws that created balance between all creatures who lived on my chest. They wanted my people to follow their way. It was all so confusing. They took my children. The moniyaw that took them away did not understand the laws of kindness and caring, love and sharing. My people grieved. The tears flowed; their hearts were broken. No longer could the elders teach the sacred laws of harmony passed to them by our Creator. No longer did the young ones run and play on me, their Mother Earth. I grieved with my people.

One day another disaster was bestowed on me and my four legged, my flying, my swimming my two legged and crawling children. Big machines came rumbling down my body onto the land that was home to the Muskotuw Sakahikan Enowuk. They ripped at my body. Open sores oozed while my people watched, helpless to stop this invasion. Then the newcomers poured hot tar on the sores which turned hard and impenetrable. More machines made their way across these tar roads. Trauma was added to trauma.

It was not long before the mooniyaw drilled into my body and sucked out my blood. The pain to me was unbearable. Me and my people suffered. Soon they began ripping my tree people from my body. The animals left. Their food and shelter was no more. The noise was overwhelming. My two legged stayed in an attempt to stop the ravaging of my body, to no avail. The two-legged, who had looked after me as I had looked after them, could no longer hunt to feed their families. Their homes nestled in my forest was one day surrounded by raw dirt. There were no flowers, no trees no animals to hunt, nothing. My people were no longer the proud and happy men and women they had been for so many moons. Even many of the unborn babies did not survive to see daylight.

To this day, the newcomers continue to take the riches from my body, with little regard for my two legged, my four legged, my flying, my swimming and my crawling children.

Glossary of Aboriginal Traditional Terms and Protocols

Ceremonies- Most ceremonies offer a communal spiritual experience. The authenticity and integrity of traditional practices and beliefs are assured when an elder is present. Most ceremonies are an oral tradition passed on by community recognized elders and leaders. To honour the elder who leads the ceremony tobacco should be respectfully presented. A gift is also appreciated as he or she gifts the participants, so it is good to gift back to keep balance.

Elders-Elders may be male or female. Only the community can pass this honored title to a member in recognition of his or hers experience and wisdom garnered throughout life. When an elder speaks, it is proper protocol to listen in silence, never interrupting. Many elders have earned special 'gifts' such as intuition, insight, spiritual guidance, healing abilities or interpreting dreams or visions. The purpose of these gifts is to assist their communities in growing spiritually, physically, mentally and emotionally. Normally no one elder has all the above gifts nor can he or she perform all the different ceremonies.

Fasting-Fasting involves total renunciation of food and water for several days depending on its purpose or intent. An Elder provides the necessary ceremonial settings , condition and protocol and guides the person who is fasting.

Feasts- Many ceremonies or gatherings will end with a feast. There are specific rituals to follow depending upon the traditions of the participants. It is best to wait respectfully in silence allowing elders to perform whatever rituals are necessary first. Sacred food varies between tribes according to their local availability.

Invocation or prayer- Aboriginal people communicate with the Creator through prayers and meditation (Called sitting in silence). Prayers are offered individually or in group ceremonies. Prayers go to the same higher power whether it is called God, Creator, Yahweh, Allah or Kitchi Manitou or other names. Most meetings and special events begin with words of prayer from respected elders, our spiritual leaders or priests. Before any such event the elders are offered tobacco and asked if he or she would conduct the prayer or ceremony. A tobacco offering indicates honour for both the elder and Creator. Hunters and gatherers also offer tobacco and prayers to plants, berries, or animals before they harvested to show respect and gratitude for the food provided.

Pipes-Pipes are used in individual or group ceremonies. Owners have earned the right to carry a pipe through careful. Truthful conduct over many years. Many are gifted from another pipe carrier or elder. Prayers are carried upward through the smoke of burning plant material in the bowl of the pipe. There is no set length, design or decoration of the pipe although women's pipes are usually smaller than men's. The bowl may be made of soapstone, marble inlaid with silver, or a special red stone from quarries in the United States. The stem may be of special hollowed out local wood like chokecherry or saskatoon. Stem and bowl are detached between uses and wrapped in an individually designed pipe bag usually made of hide or cloth. It is the responsibility of the pipe carrier to respectfully care for and protect their pipe at all times,

Pipe Ceremony- The pipe ceremony is one of the basic gatherings over which an elder or pipe carrier presides. Participants usually sit in a circle in respectful silence unless invited to speak. Burning of sweetgrass or smudging is used to purify each and every one present before further proceedings. The elder places tobacco in the bowl of his pipe. Then offers the pipe to each of the four directions. and the four sacred medicine powers associated with each direction. Animal spirit guides are similar to guardian angels in the Christian belief. The pipe is passed clockwise to every person around the circle to smoke and add their own prayers in silence. A pipe ceremony is a silent, sacred experience Once completed the elder or pipe carrier may hold it up in offering to all creation, to the spirit helpers, to the Creator. Any remains in the pipe bowl will later be returned to Mother Earth with a prayer of gratitude for sharing Her bounty.

The meeting is now open.

Pow-wows-Pow wowing is a way of life all through the summer. Everyone from all over Canada and the United States gather for dancing, feasting, competing, laughing, teasing and remembering the old traditions and catching up on the latest news of extended family and friends. It returns pride of culture and traditions back to Aboriginal people. Sobriety is a well-established standard strictly enforced by security officials. Drinking or abusing drugs during a pow wow is not tolerated.

Each powwow may have as many as one thousand dancers. Each are a member of a family group and generally camp at the grounds. Visitors from all over the globe also congregate for the powwows.

Each powwow begins with a grand entry, led by the eagle staff and then the flags of the various countries and tribes represented. Following will be elders and honored guests, and then all the dancers in their bright colors come in by categories. So many dancers wearing such colorful and meaningful regalia is a sight to behold. Each grand entry honours the drums, the flags, all our veterans and the VIPs like the chiefs and even some politicians. And it is all lead by the elder's prayers.

There is dancing for healing, for honoring the hunters, for celebrations of the past. For honoring the scouts who went first when the camps moved There are honour dances for people, there are initiation ceremonies to welcome a new dancer into the powwow trail. There are give-away ceremonies. There are ceremonies for picking up a dropped feather, there are eagle whistle ceremonies and above all there is much drumming and dancing, eating and visiting and just a wonderful time is had at the powwows.

Each dancer dances for a purpose.

Smudging for Purification- A smudge uses one or several sacred plants. They may be placed in an abalone seashell (to represent the four elements of earth, air fire and water)and then lit to create first a fire and then a smoking smudge. Dancers and drummers smudge themselves and their sacred items before beginning a ceremony or dance. Smudging for purification is done before most ceremonies or meetings in the Native community. After removing glasses and jewelry each participant is invited to draw the smoke four times toward their face, head heart and body, praying silently for purification and truth to come to them. Some pass the smoke over the ears, eyes, mouth and heart so the individual may hear the truth, see the truth, speak the truth and know the truth in his or her heart respectively. The smudge is silently carried clockwise to every participant and then back to the elder. No judgement is made to those who decline the smudging.

Sweatlodge- This ceremony is the Aboriginal way of symbolically returning to the womb of Mother Earth for purification and renewal. Our mother feeds and nurtures us into the world in the purity of our beginnings. - pure in body. Mind. Heart and spirit. A sweat lodge ceremony is a new beginning. Using agents of Mother Earth such as rocks and water, participants enter a dome-shaped structure made of willow poles, buffalo robes or canvas and blankets. Rocks are heated in a fire outside the lodge, then carefully carried into a deep hole in the middle of the lodge. Once the doorway is sealed into complete darkness water is poured over the rocks and special herbs to create a healing steam.

This ceremony from beginning to end is accompanied by prayer and song to revitalize a strength, a power, the connection we have with Mother Earth. It is a time of personal meditation, prayer. Purification, cleansing, releasing and communal support.

Sweetgrass, cedar sage and tobacco- These four sacred plants are easily available across North America. They are used individually or in combination in ceremonies. They are burned like incense for the purification and the coming together of many hearts and minds as one. This is a widespread daily private practice for those who are deeply involved in Aboriginal spirituality.

Sundance- Held during the summer solstice, this dance was in honour of women. The men gave themselves to Mother Earth as warriors. It included four days of dancing, fasting for the dancers and prayers from all who attended. They prayed for the good health of all 'our relations, which includes all the people plants and animals of the Earth.

Spiritual Objects

Eagle Feathers. Are awarded for outstanding deeds of courage, valour, determination, leadership or wisdom. The eagle is considered a powerful, sacred bird because he flies the highest and therefore has the closest connection to Creator. He represents strength, power , loyalty and vision.

Drums-Drums are the heartbeat of the Nation. There are many types of drums. Each one is considered a sacred object ansd should never be touched without proper protocol to the carrier. One should not reach across it or place anything on it.

Rattles- are shaken to call the spirit of life, which takes care of human beings. During a sweatlodge ceremony an elder may use it to invite spirits of the four directions.to enter and help participants seeking a spiritual and physical cleansing, in order to start a new life. The rattle is also used to doctor people.

Glossary of political terms

Treaties- A treaty, according to international law is an agreement, a contract or a truce between two or more sovereign states. The purpose of the treaties between Canada, the Crown and First Nations from the government's perspective was to acquire land for settlement and make First Nations wards of the Crown with the intention of transitioning the people into a new economy. First Nations people thought the treaties had benefits for their communities and were intended to foster good relations and sharing of land between themselves, the Crown and all the people in Canada. These were large areas where both Native and non-native people lived. For instance, most of Alberta is divided into three distinct treaty areas. The south is 7,central is 6 and northern is 8.

Indian Act-The Indian Act is not a treaty, and is different from the treaties in that it is the legal response to the treaties. It is the governments way of enforcing their interpretation of what they decide the purpose of the treaties are.

Reservations-specified by the Indian Act as a tract of land, the legal title to which is vested in Her Majesty that has been set apart for the use and benefit of a band. Each treaty area will have many reservations. Although the treaties were meant to protect, they have resulted in many restrictions. One is the inability to borrow money, even for a home, as it left the lending institutions without being able to re-posses property which was in default. Trade out of the reserve was not allowed.

Band-A band is a group of people who resided together in a certain place, the same as a community. People were restricted to the small tracts of land allocated, the reservations. They may be comprised of large family groups of the same ethnicity and language. Some got mixed when they happened to be camped in the same area.

Caveat-A formal notice filed with a court or officer to suspend proceeding until filer is given a hearing. We filed to keep companies off our land until the disputes were settled. Government disallowed it.

Timeline

1872	Manifest destiny developed by Father Lacombe stating it was Gods plan that the European Christians come to North America to save the souls of the Native people.
1876	Indian Act became law governing all treaty Indians and designated land.
1880	Arrival of the Hudson Bay
1884	Mandated Residential school. All treaty children removed from parents.
1903	Henry's mother born
1918	Spanish flue hit Lubicon area. Those who used traditional medicine survived.
1925	Amendment to Indian Act forbidding gatherings, sacred practices and hiring a Lawyer or form political associations.
1939	Indian Association formed despite it being illegal. It went on to be a powerful lobby group for Indian rights
1939	Grouard Residential School opened.

1940	Henry was born.
1944	Baptism at Lubicon Lake. Divided community.
1947	Henry's kidnapping
1951	Ceremonies and gatherings made legal again. We could now access legal advice and fight for our rights in court.
1953	Henry hits priest and leaves residential school
1959	Loon Lake healing. Loon Lake stayed traditional and took nothing from the Whites.
1960	Indians got the vote for the first time. Divided communities. Not all knew.
1962	Grouard residential school was closed.
1963	Henry's people were notified of their right to vote.
1968	Henry married
1969	White Paper introduced proposing breakup of reserves.
1969	Counter proposal with the Red Paper. Government backed down.
1969	Dept of Indian affairs took over residential schools. Abuse and separation continued.
1970	Began Alternative Action Program in the north which focused on proper western education and a return to traditional teachings.
1971-1973	Government built all-weather road into Lubicon lands without consultation.
1974	Lubicon members patronized to their own reserve.
1975	Oil companies moved in and polluted water ways, air and land. Still no consultation or compensation

1980	AVC opened in Grouard and they offered the Education Technicians Program
1983	400 oil and gas wells open within 25km radius of of the Lubicon settlement. In an 18-month period out of 21 pregnancies, only two live births.
1983	9/10 people on welfare compared 1/10 in 1979
1984	Federal study 90% drop in meat and furs harvest.
1987	United Nations human rights commission report released condemning the Canadian government.
1989	Diashawa, a Japanese lumber company granted lumber rights. Still no consultation or compensation.
1994	US based Unical built sour gas plant close to community.
1996	Last Residential School closed.
1999	Northern College developed, and Affirmative Action Program closed.
2002	Henry taught culture for Aboriginal Diabetes Wellness program
2003	Amnesty International report complete. Concluded Rights of Native people violated and felt they could not get justice from the Canadian government.
2006	Henry received residential school settlement and bought new truck and camping trailer.
2018 April 14	Henry ended his earth journey
2018 Oct. 24th	Lubicon land claim settlement

Lightning Source UK Ltd.
Milton Keynes UK
UKHW041329101122
411975UK00007B/160